Advance Praise for

THE SPLENDOR OF CREATION

"Our thanks to Bernstein, birth-mother of the Jewish environmental movement, for this very personal book. She seamlessly weaves together Genesis and contemporary environmental awareness, forming a union in which each of these turns out to be the deeper meaning of the other. A very honest, down-to-earth, and sometimes profound reflection."

—Rabbi Arthur Green, dean,
The Rabbinical School at Hebrew College,
Newton Centre, Massachusetts

"As someone with no religious affiliation, I found Bernstein's brilliant and inspired interpretation of Genesis riveting. I never realized that the Bible could offer insight to me as an environmentalist, but *The Splendor of Creation* convinces me that a reverence for nature is rooted in the Bible."

—Peter Barnes, co-founder of
Working Assets and author of
Who Owns the Sky?

"This book bears the mark of a life work—careful thought, spiritual insights, deep reflection on the meaning of a biblical text. It is a genre of writing very difficult to do well, combining scholarship with poetry and autobiography. In love with the language of the Bible, Bernstein has been thinking and speaking and teaching for most of her adult life, seeking to inspire Jews to respect the earth and to live in harmony with it. For decades, she has been on a journey to write this important book that readers will want to share with others because she has dared to trust them with the intimacy of her heart."

—Eli N. Evans, author of
*The Provincials: A Personal History
of Jews in the South*

THE SPLENDOR OF CREATION

A BIBLICAL ECOLOGY

Ellen Bernstein

THE PILGRIM PRESS   CLEVELAND

DEDICATION

*This book is dedicated to my beloved community
of Mt. Airy, which nurtures me every day,*

and in particular to

Germantown Jewish Centre and its minyanim:
Dorshei Derech and Masorti

Weaver's Way Coop

Wissahickon Creek and all of its inhabitants

In loving memory of

Rabbi Joseph B. Glaser ẓ"l

Rabbi Daniel Kamesar ẓ"l

The Pilgrim Press, 700 Prospect Avenue, Cleveland, Ohio 44115-1100
thepilgrimpress.com

© 2005 by Ellen Bernstein

All rights reserved. Published 2005

Printed in the United States of America on acid-free paper

10   09   08   07   06   05   5   4   3   2

Library of Congress Cataloging-in-Publication Data

Bernstein, Ellen, 1953–
      The splendor of creation : a biblical ecology / Ellen Bernstein.
         p.   cm.
      Includes bibliographical references.
      ISBN 0-8298-1664-X (paper : alk. paper)
         1. Nature—Biblical teaching.   2. Human ecology—Biblical teaching.
3. Bible. O.T. Genesis—Criticism, interpretation, etc.   Nature—Religious
aspects—Judaism.   5. Human ecology—Religious aspects—Judaism.   I.
Title.

BS1199.N34B47   2005
296.3'8—dc22

                                                        2005042986

CONTENTS

ACKNOWLEDGMENTS

This book has a long and windy history. It began as an idea that captured my imagination fourteen years ago during my tenure as founder and director of Shomrei Adamah, Keepers of the Earth, the first Jewish environmental organization. The original plan was to develop a curriculum that used Genesis 1 as a model text for teaching people how to read the Bible from an ecological perspective. I am eternally grateful to Judith Ginsberg, Eli Evans, and the Covenant Foundation for believing in me and providing a major grant to develop the initial material. I am also grateful to Dr. Gavriel Goldman, who worked with me on the preliminary curriculum, and to Josh Meyer for his artwork and Sheila Segal for her editing of that early work.

I always believed that the ideas in Genesis 1 had universal appeal and deserved a medium that could transcend the limitations of a curriculum and deliver the language, poetry, beauty, and wisdom of Genesis to a wider audience. I committed myself to the task of bringing the text alive and the result is this volume, *The Splendor of Creation: A Biblical Ecology*.

Numerous people helped in myriad ways to bring this project to fruition—it took more than a village. Undoubtedly this list overlooks someone; however, please know that your efforts did not go unnoticed. I am grateful to the Arad Arts Project, Peter Barnes and the Mesa Refuge, Thomas Berry, Caron Chess, Rabbi Rachel Cowan, James Cummings, Ruth Sorenson Cummings and the Nathan Cummings Foundation, Jeffrey Dekro, Irene Diamond, John Elder, Stephany Evans, Rachel Falcove, David Ferleger, Ellen Frankel, Jonathan Friedan, Rabbi Dayle Friedman, Ellen Friedman, Jeff Garson, Terry Gips, Natalie Goldfein, Rabbi Leonard Gordon, Jonathan Harmon, Bert Harmon and the Henry Levy Discretionary Trust, Anna Herman, Rabbi Hayim Herring, Sue Hoffman, John Hunting, Victoria Jenkins, Estherelke Kaplan, John Keogh, Linda Kriger, Rabbi Harold Kushner, Arthur Kurzweil, Rick Lederman, Herbie Levine, Deanna Mayer, John Powers and the Educational Foundation of America, Bernie Pucker, Steven Rockefeller, Rabbi Norbert Samuelson, Rabbi Zalman Schacter-Shalomi, Mindy Shapiro, Steve Tobias, Hooper Brooks, Ed Skloot and the Surdna Foundation, Rabbi Arthur Waskow, Adam Werbach, the faculty and staff of the Reconstructionist Rabbinical College and library, and Kim Sadler, Kris Firth, Frederick Porter, and the staff of The Pilgrim Press.

Special thanks to Gina Michaels, Rabbi Marsha Pik Nathan, and Rabbi Gershon Winkler, who went way beyond the call of duty to read and edit this book.

Shomrei Adamah Board members Rabbi Mordechai Liebling, Mimi Schneirov, Evie Berger, and Rabbi Joseph Glaser z"l, were a constant source of support to me over the years, and the members of Shomrei Adamah were my inspiration.

Miki Young and Rabbi Rami Shapiro acted as midwives to this work and spent countless hours reading and rereading the text, arguing with me about it and offering invaluable feedback. Without their abiding love and encouragement, this book would not have seen the light of day.

—*Ellen Bernstein*
Wissahickon River Valley, Philadelphia
Hanukkah, 5764, 2003
ellen.bernstein@verizon.net

INTRODUCTION

At the core of the environmental crisis is a great divide between mind and body, between head and heart, between human and nature. This divide is not new. The world's religions and mythologies have always told stories of humanity's separation from nature. But today the split is so vast that its consequences on the environment are potentially catastrophic.

The Jewish mystics of the seventeenth century said that when Adam and Eve ate the apple from the tree of knowledge of good and evil, they set in motion the rift between humanity and nature.

In the beginning, the world was whole and the creatures knew their place. Adam and Eve lived a peaceable life in the Garden of Eden. God had invited Adam to enjoy all of the fruits of the Garden —except for the fruit of the tree of knowledge. "If you eat from it, you will surely die."

Adam and Eve ate the apple from the tree of knowledge. They let themselves be seduced into thinking that the knowledge tree would bring them superior powers; that knowing more would mean being more. They challenged the original order and goodness of the universe by taking something that was not theirs to take. The fruit of the tree of knowledge was God's sacred property. It was not for people to eat or use.

Adam and Eve did not die a bodily death for their transgression (at least not immediately), but they did die a spiritual one. They were expelled from paradise and condemned to a life of suffering. They would be alienated from each other and the land for the rest of their lives. In taking what was not theirs, they upset the balance of nature and ruptured their own interior balance.

We choose a path that leads to spiritual death and nature's ruin whenever we take what is not ours, whenever we believe that our portion is not enough, whenever we assume that knowledge is a commodity we can consume.

Yet, just as we have the power to spoil the creation, we also have the power to make it whole. We have the power to mend the earth and to mend ourselves, to sew the pieces back together again.

Mending the earth and our selves demands sustenance and vision. It is a lifelong task. It requires lifelong love. I have chosen Judaism as the path I walk and the Bible as the sacred text I contemplate along the path. I offer them up to you in *The Splendor of Creation*.

As a child in New England in the 1950s and 1960s, playing in nature was my raison d'etre. My life revolved around outings of all kinds: canoe trips, mountain climbing, bike adventures and rambles through the woods. I loved the feeling of being all tuckered out from a day well spent in the fresh air.

I was grateful to have an opportunity to pursue my love of nature in high school through an innovative program in environmental science. Each week we would visit various sites along the Ashuelot River in southern New Hampshire to determine the health of the river. Like real scientists, we waded out in the water to measure dissolved oxygen and various pollution indicators with our new Hach Kits. I was hooked on this emerging field of environmental studies and followed my interests throughout college.

My love for nature grew deeper as I watched it disappear before my eyes: forest clear-cut, rivers dammed, farms gobbled up. I feared for nature. In my own life, nothing was more central, but most people seemed unmoved by this destruction. They did not see what I saw.

I was frightened that we were destroying our Earth in vain attempts to aggrandize ourselves and I wanted in some way to transmit to others my sense of the preciousness of nature. When I graduated college, I taught high school biology. But the scientific information I tried to impart was not enough to motivate my students to care. Facts and figures got in the way of love and meaning, of genuine connection.

So I abandoned the traditional textbooks and, instead, introduced my students to the great nature writers. I designed a curriculum to teach various ecological and biological concepts using the stories of Annie Dillard, Loren Eiseley, Aldo Leopold. It worked; my students were captivated. The stories were the flesh and blood experiences that could bring the dry scientific bones to life. Stories and personal experiences, I discovered, find their way into the body and the heart, into the places that "information" alone will never go; and they stick. Learning becomes effortless through stories.

While I was teaching, I was on my own spiritual quest. I understood my relationship with nature as a kind of religion and I wanted to see what wisdom I could find from sacred texts. I had left behind the lackluster Judaism of my youth and had experimented with a variety of eastern practices and paths, but thought that I should revisit the Hebrew Bible to see if perhaps I might have missed something in my childhood. Reading the Bible afresh with ecologist's eyes, I was amazed to find the distinguished place that nature holds in the stories, poetry, celebrations, holidays, law, and prayers.

I realized that ecology and the Bible were using different languages to describe the same thing. The Bible and ecology both teach humility, modesty, kindness to all beings, a reverence for life, and a concern for future generations. They both teach that the earth is sacred and mysterious. They both describe an interconnected universe, bound together through invisible threads. They both speak of life flowing in spirals and cycles and hold that all actions—no matter how small—yield consequences.

I began to see churches and synagogues, which hold the Bible sacred, as natural places to raise ecological consciousness. If you consider the fact that the Bible is still the most widely read book in the world, touching the lives of millions of people every day, and that it has served humanity as a guide for living for the past three thousand years, it becomes clear that religious institutions could take a powerful leadership role in environmental repair. If churches and synagogues could teach people to read the Bible with ecological eyes and see spirituality in ecological terms, then we'd have a built-in infrastructure for expanding environmental awareness and practice. And since religious institutions also strive to teach people to "care," I dreamed that maybe they could inspire their congregants to care for nature.

My passion for nature and religion led me, with much trepidation, to start the first national Jewish environmental organization, Shomrei Adamah, "Keepers of the Earth." I had never been involved in organizational life before, had little knowledge of Judaism, and knew nothing about the established Jewish community (indeed, I was still pretty ambivalent about my own Judaism).

For ten years I worked with rabbis, scientists, environmentalists, and writers around the country to create educational materials that would bring to life the ecological dimensions of the Bible and Judaism. We developed books and curricula that rabbis and educators could use with their congregants to illuminate the "natural" side of Jewish holidays, stories, ethics, law, and practices.

Even though the work was successful, I felt it was limited in its ability to reach a wide audience. And perhaps more important, I felt I had not fully articulated my own ecological vision.

Having long before witnessed the power of stories to transform the attitudes of my students, I imagined that one of the Bible's most popular stories, Genesis 1, could have the potential to reach a broad audience and open peoples' hearts to nature.

The Genesis narrative was so familiar that for years I would just breeze through it. But even a surface reading yields ecological significance. Genesis 1 recounts the seven days and seven categories of creation: light on day one, air on the second day, waters and earth on the third day. Once the elemental habitats are created, their inhabitants move in: waters give rise to swimming creatures, air gives rise to flying creatures, and earth gives rise to walking creatures. The story is beautiful. Its lyricism and poetry eloquently express a sense of wholeness and a reverence for nature. I realized that Genesis 1 is indeed the Western world's first environmental epic.

As I rooted around in the text, I discovered several ecospiritual themes embedded within: the mystery of creation, the goodness of nature, the power of limits, the importance of diversity and sustainability, the ecology of time, the balance of work and rest, the interdependence of everything, and a sense of place, order, and harmony.

I also recognized mystical and mythic dimensions of the creations: soul is created on day one, intellect on the second day, emotions and actions on the third, time on the fourth, movement on the fifth, love and work on the sixth, and rest and eternity on the seventh. Genesis speaks to our inner nature, as well as to our outer nature.

Inspired by the text, I committed myself to the task of illuminating its deep ecological message for others. This book, *The Splendor of Creation*, is my midrash—a story about a story—on creation. To help me with my task, I have explored the teachings of my own tradition, the writings of the rabbis, as well as the wisdom of scientists, philosophers, and poets through the ages. One of the great rewards of investigating ancient texts is finding what you thought were your own original ideas, clearly articulated by people who lived hundreds or thousands of years ago. Two rabbis in particular provided special guidance for me: Nachmanides (Rabbi Moshe ben Nachman), a thirteenth-century Spanish scholar, philosopher, physician, and poet, a Renaissance man who brought a kabbalistic or mystical orientation to the text, and Samson Raphael Hirsch, a nineteenth-century German Orthodox rabbi who expressed an uncanny ecological perspective.

Today, as I write, the words of Rabbi Bahya ibn Pakuda, an eleventh-century Jewish philosopher, ring in my ears: "Meditation on creation is obligatory," he said. "You should try to understand both the smallest and greatest of God's creatures. Examine carefully those which are hidden from you."[1]

It is the pleasure and the work of each generation to bring the Bible to life. My job is to breathe new light into the very first chapter. This book considers the mysteries of creation and offers back a reverence for life and a creation ethic. In the end the earth will become whole as we become whole, when we see nature as integral to our identities and stewardship as an extension of our everyday lives.

I

L I G H T

THE FIRST DAY

In the beginning God
created the heaven and the earth.

The earth was desolate and void and
darkness was over the face of the deep,
and the breath of God hovered
over the surface of the water.

And God said, "Let there be light";
and there was light.

And God saw the light was good,
and God made a division
between the light and the darkness.

And God called the light: "Day!"
and God called the darkness: "Night!"
And there was evening and
there was morning, one day.

꙳

In the beginning, **God created** the heaven and the earth. (1.1)

*Be-raishit **bara Elohim** et ha-shamayim ve-et ha-aretz.*

꙳

THE MYSTERY OF CREATION

The idea that a God exists who created heaven and earth is truly profound. It means that the earth that we walk upon, the air that we breathe, the food that we eat, are all signs that the world is filled with mystery. Those who cherish this idea sense that everything they encounter is sacred. Nurture this idea, and it will guide the choices you make and the way you live your life.

For most of us, the idea that our land, waters, and air are manifestations of the Sacred has disappeared from our mental vocabulary. We point to it in other cultures—Native American and Buddhist—but we have forgotten that it exists in our own biblical tradition.

Many of us have lost this idea, in part, because we're estranged from nature. We think of nature as inert stuff without any life of its own; we approach it merely as a tool to achieve human ends. In a world in which we are divided from nature, in which we recognize nature for its economic value only, land becomes "real estate" and trees "timber." It is no wonder we have become oblivious to the sacredness of the world.

Many years ago, I realized that God was the overlooked dimension of the environmental equation. As a forever-in-the-woods tomboy who found adventure and solace in nature, I believed that all of nature had a purpose and that all creatures had value whether or not I could know that value. My experiences in wilderness often overwhelmed me with feelings of grandeur and mystery. A random universe made no sense for me, given the extraordinary beauty of the world. If all these creatures belonged here and had distinct purpose, there must be a Creator.

As I grew older I nurtured my interests in nature through studies in biology and ecology. But the deeper I delved, the more I realized that science approached environment as a problem to solve rather than a mystery to revere. If I wanted to experience the mystery of Nature, I would have to make room for the mystery inside myself. I began, with some trepidation, to explore the possibility of living with God in my life.

My seeking initially took place in my mind. I liked the idea that a spiritual life, a God-centered life, could provide the antidote to the "me-centeredness" and the consumer orientation that define our culture and threaten our environment. While a primary goal of an American life is to make money to buy "things," the primary goal of a spiritual life is to make time for no-"thing," for that which money can't buy: for God, mystery, conversation, ideas, passion, nature, soul. While the deafening voice of the marketplace drives us to get rich, get smart, get beautiful, advance, achieve, buy, the still small voice of a spiritual life delights in long walks in the woods, regular periods of silence, and hearty meals with friends. Adopting a spiritual life, a God-centered life, could be the most difficult and radical step one could take towards creating more ecologically sustainable world.

A God-centered life is not about leaving the world and nature. Quite the contrary. It means finding ways to engage in life and nature more deeply, with all of the senses. We have been trained to read the world with our heads only, as if our bodies, hearts, and senses had nothing to do with it. In the process we split our minds from our bodies and our bodies from the world, and we lose touch with a whole domain of sensual and intuitive knowledge. Even the word "environment" is so intellectual, removed from the textures, smells, and colors of the living world—abstracted from its beauty. A God-centered life is a fitting response to a world that devalues nature itself, while it overvalues the "things" we take from nature.

Seeking God became for me the ultimate ecological expression. But it is one thing to accept the idea of God in my mind, and quite another to let the presence of God penetrate my being, take root in my body, and inform my feelings and behaviors—for God to be alive in my heart.

If I could actually live this reality, that God created heaven and earth, then my life would be enriched with the miraculousness of everything. I would know deeply that the world is founded in generosity and love. I would give more than I would take; I would be more compassionate, less judgmental, more aware that all of my actions, even all of my thoughts, have repercussions in the mysterious round of life.

And if all people could remember this and act on their awareness, then I imagine we would finally learn how to care for the world.

If God exists in everything and everyone, if the world and everything it holds is sacred, then we have no choice but to find and lift up the godly sparks in all of life. According to the Jewish mystics when the world was created, God poured light into the original unformed mass, forming ten etheric vessels. But the vessels were not strong enough to contain the light and they shattered, leaving the shards of the vessels embedded in the matter of the world. It is our task, in the language of the Jewish mystics, to retrieve the shards of the holy vessels and put the pieces back together again.

Nothing could be more difficult, really, than taking God seriously. If we were to accept the presence of God in our lives, we would walk more quietly, eat more deliberately, take time for loving each other, and act with curiosity and sensitivity to all things. We would treat the whole world as a gift.

Genesis 1.1 tells us this. The whole world is holy because God created it and is alive within it. It is an idea that is so powerful, that if we are open to it, it can lead us to an ecological vision and guide us toward ecological lives. It lays the foundation for a deep environmental ethic, a creation ethic.

✦

❧

The earth was **desolate and void** and
darkness was over the surface of the deep
and the **breath of God hovered** over the surface of the water.[1] (1.2)

*Ve-ha-aretz hayetah **tohu va-vohu***
ve-choshekh al-penai tehom
*ve-**ruach Elohim merachefet** al penai ha-mayim.*

❧

THE BEGINNING

The beginning of the universe is characterized by *tohu va-vohu*, chaos and confusion, a swirling emptiness, a black hole. Even the sounds of the Hebrew words suggest a mysterious void. The early biblical commentators understood *tohu va-vohu* as the primeval energy of the universe. It contained the potential for all that would be created. Given the right catalyst, the energy of *tohu va-vohu* could transform into matter. From this initial chaos, everything that ever existed or would exist was formed.[2]

The catalyst for this transformation from *tohu va-vohu* to matter is God. God's breath "hovers" over the waters. *Merachefet*, the Hebrew word for "hover," is often associated with a nesting mother eagle who carefully shields and nurtures her young. So too, God's hovering offers a sense of protection and devotion. Simply by breathing, *ruach Elohim*, God whispers love into every molecule of the turbulent water.

The current scientific idea about the "beginning" echoes the biblical one. According to cosmologists, a mysterious catalyst instigated the process of life. In 1945, Russian-born geologist George Gamow theorized that the universe had emerged from a "primordial fireball," a burst of pure and concentrated energy. He claimed there was a particular moment, a "big bang" or a "flaring forth" (to quote theologian Thomas Berry) when the universe, as we know it, came into being. The big bang theory was further corroborated in 1964 when two scientists, studying the radiation characteristics of space, recognized some low-level "noise" emanating throughout the sky. Physicists determined that this noise was a reverberation of the big bang that had occurred billions of years ago.

The picture of the early universe, according to most modern scientists, resembled the *tohu va-vohu* of the Bible. They believe that all the mass and energy of the universe was concentrated into an infinitely small point and squeezed to an infinitely high density. All of the mass and energy that would ever be was there in the beginning. It was a dark and hot, fiery brew of colliding photons and free electrons. The gravity generated by this mass was so great that nothing could escape. Not even light.

Then an explosion occurred that forced the energy-matter outward in all directions and the material universe came into being. Astrophysicists cannot explain why matter began to flow outward, but early in the life of our universe, they suggest a one-time new type of expansionary force, an "inflationary epoch," or in the language of Genesis, "an exhalation of God."[3]

Over the next several hundred thousand years, as the temperature fell to 3000 degrees Kelvin, electrons bound up in stable orbits around hydrogen and helium nuclei and photons separated out from the darkness of the universe. And then there was light.

꙳

And God said "Let there be **light**;" and there was **light**. (1.3)

*Va-yomer Elohim yehi **or** va-yehi-**or**.*

꙳

THE LIGHT OF THE SOUL

Light is the first creation; it is the essence of life. The ancient rabbis speculated that the original light was unique and awesome, brighter and more powerful than sunlight (which was created on the fourth day). They supposed that this first light was so bright that there was no darkness or night. One rabbi said the primordial light illuminated the most minute, normally invisible particles. Another maintained that by this light you could see across the entire universe.

The ancients thought that the original light was the light of awareness, the light that ignites and orders creation. The Hebrew word for light, *or*, is similar to the Hebrew word for awake, *orr*. Light calls all matter to awaken and unfold.[4]

Light is luminous and radiant: it dazzles, emanates, flows, waves, and jumps. It defies definition and constraint; it cannot be captured or contained. Because of its elusive nature, the rabbis said that the phrase, "it was so," which they interpreted as "it was established," is curiously absent from the first day (it appears on every other). "Established" implies a sense of a concrete reality, but light is not concrete; it is pure energy.

A midrash teaches that all souls were created on day one.[5] "The soul of man is the lamp of God" sang Solomon. Our souls are like vessels for God, designed to receive God's light and shine it forth. Through the light of our souls we are bound to God, to each other, and to the soul of the world.

God's light is so strong we can't receive it directly; it would destroy our bodies. It is funneled from on high through a ladder of five higher souls, diminishing in intensity at each rung, until it reaches us at a level that our bodies can contain.[6]

Our soul's light is always accessible to us, even though it seems elusive and we lose touch with it time and again. It is the fire in our belly, our driving energy, our enthusiasm and passion. It can burn brightly, keeping us warm and alive like the burning bush, which was never consumed; it is our ecstasy, our wildness, our spark of divinity. It can also burst out of control like volcanoes or lightning or forest fires, devouring everything in sight. According to Jewish mysticism, when we are in touch with our souls, we enter the realm of *atzilut*; a closeness to God.

Still, the soul's light is subtle; it requires care. We need to tend the fire to keep it burning. Following our hearts and feelings enhances the flame. Submitting to the "shoulds" of our heads diminishes it.

Most of us aren't aware of the myriad ways that we sacrifice our light to the gods of rationalism, secularism, scientism, and consumerism in return for the illusion of control, security, and comfort. Society encourages us to submit to these idols, so we sell our souls. We grow dark and separate from ourselves. A "lost soul" is one whose soul no longer even resides within; it roams the ethers, tethered to the body by only a thread.

Without our own inner light to sustain us, we may seek energy and stimulation in the wrong places. My friend Susan describes how she realized in midlife that she had an "adrenalin addiction." She would find jobs or relationships that produced an enormous amount of excitement, tension, and fear and kept her constantly on fire. She had somehow lost touch with her soul-light, her one reliable source of energy, and had to create impossible emotional adventures to ignite her passion. Separated from our soul-light, we spend a lot of energy scurrying around to fill ourselves up, and we have little to give back to the world.

Losing touch with our souls is a subtle process that begins in the embryo. A midrash teaches that a bright light shines over us in the womb illuminating the past and the future so that we can know all that was and all that will be. But before we are born, we get angry and wrestle with an angel of God, who responds by taking away the light and hiding it. We end up forgetting all we once knew and spend the rest of our lives looking for the light.[7]

We need to remember this: that light is elusive and hidden. Discovering it and recovering it is part of our ongoing life's work.

﹏

God **saw** the light was good,
and God made a division between the light and the darkness. (1.4)

*Va-**yar** Elohim et-ha-or ki-tov*
va-yavdail Elohim bain ha-or u-vain ha-choshekh.

﹏

THE ART OF SEEING

The kabbalists believed that seeing is a creative act. They said that an object becomes visible when the eye sends out a stream of energy. The see-er, in effect, collaborates with what is being seen.[8] What we see is affected by how we see.

It is said that "our eyes are the window of our souls." Our eyes allow others to catch a glimpse of our souls, and our souls see the world through our eyes. When our eyes are connected to our souls, then we see the beauty and goodness of nature and life.

When we're disconnected from the light of our souls, the world around us appears unremarkable. We grow up amidst the most astounding riches, surrounded by the most fantastic creations, but it's easy to lose sight of the everyday miracles if we're separate from ourselves. If we aren't letting in light, we become dull, and the world becomes dull in our eyes.

Some of us need the exotic and the unfamiliar to actually see creation. We go on lavish vacations to faraway places to help us to open our eyes. We are more intrigued by the creatures and peoples on the other side of the earth than the ones in our own backyard. Foreign adventures can provide the momentary jolt to help us change our perspective and open up to the light, but it is possible to have the same sense of aliveness to the world in our own neighborhoods.

When we see with our souls, we can see what we never saw before. Annie Dillard writes:

> There are lots of things to see: unwrapped gifts and free surprises. The world is fairly studded and strewn with pennies cast broadside from a generous hand. But—and this is the point—who gets excited by a mere penny? It is dire poverty indeed when a man is so malnourished and fatigued that he won't stoop to pick up a penny. But if you cultivate a healthy poverty and simplicity so that finding a penny will literally make your day, then, since the world is in fact planted in pennies, you have with your poverty bought a lifetime of days.[9]

It takes some practice, but it's mostly a matter of quieting our minds and letting ourselves "be." The more you see, the more you get.

There are times when it's difficult for me to see. I find it especially hard when I'm angry, depressed, irritable, or preoccupied, when I've lost touch with the light of my soul. If my heart is shut down, so are my eyes. I can't recognize the goodness outside when I'm preoccupied inside.

But on good days, I see beauty everywhere. When I drive along Kelly Drive into Philadelphia, there's a surprise around every bend. I don't care if I encounter traffic—it gives me more time to contemplate the river, to look out for gay daffodils, to admire the granite outcroppings, and to watch the scullers row. I'm not concerned with naming all the plants or explaining how the rock formations arose. I feel invigorated just seeing the colors, shapes, and textures of water, rock, and tree against a backdrop of regal skyscrapers.

And it's not just the natural beauty that's so magical. Sculpture gardens, architectural treasures, and history enrich the experience of my commute. I try to remember all the people who made this green corridor what it is today. I am grateful to the early city planners such as William Penn, who had a vision of a "greene country towne;" and to the Philadelphia Watering Committee, who purchased large estates along the river to preserve the purity of the water; and to the Pennsylvania General Assembly, who established the greenway along the river "forever as an open public place." These early planners knew that parks were critical to the health and the livelihood of a city and its people.

When we recognize the beauty and the mystery in everything, the whole world can become enchanted. The sense of beauty can provide a profound support for our work in the world. "Let the beauty we love be what we do," wrote the poet Rumi. "There are hundreds of ways to kneel and kiss the ground."[10]

❧

And God called the light "Day!" and God called the darkness "Night!"
And there was **evening** and there was **morning**, one day. (1.5)

Va-yikra Elohim la-or yom ve-la-choshekh kara laylah
Va-yehi-erev va-yehi-voker yom echad.

❧

THE PRIMARY RHYTHM OF DARKNESS AND LIGHT

The pattern of night and day introduced an element of order to the primeval chaos. Day and night—light and dark—established a cyclical rhythm and laid a foundation for time, the infrastructure for all life on earth. Light and dark each have their own special functions: light stimulates activity and growth, darkness promotes rest and renewal. Plants photosynthesize by day and rest by night. Some animals hunt and gather by day and rest and digest by night. Most people work and create by day and relax and sleep at night. All creatures are calibrated by the rhythm of day and night.

"All life begins and is nurtured in the womb of darkness," wrote Samson Raphael Hirsch. "Everything matures under the rays of light. Light could not work ceaselessly; no creature could bear it."[11]

Genesis does not say "and there was night and there was day." Rather, it says "and there was evening/*erev*, and morning/*voker*." The root of *erev* refers to the blurring of boundaries, while *voker* alludes to clarity and distinctions. *Erev* corresponds to chaos and *voker* to order. This phrase is repeated each day. Every day, the world goes through another round of chaos and order. Every day we are reminded of the essential cycle of creation. Both light and darkness, order and chaos, are critical to the fabric of life.

The Jewish convention of starting the twenty-four-hour day with evening, followed by morning, is derived from this verse. We might assume the reverse: that daytime, when we take control, should start the cycle. But this pattern of evening giving way to morning reflects the primary rhythm of the universe: chaos precedes order.

We rarely honor the dark times of our own lives: the winter, the night, the hours of uncertainty and confusion, the dark night of the soul. We tend to value our "light" phase and dismiss the rest. It's important to remember that the universe was created out of darkness. We need darkness for rest and receiving, for the development of our souls, for the mystery of life to deepen inside of us.

If we disparage our own darkness, we also demean the chaos of the natural world. Indeed, society tries to overcompensate for our shared discomfort by imposing more and more order on nature. We turn tangled woods into housing developments and electrically light up the night, embossing our human imprint everywhere and disturbing the essential rhythm of life.

Jungian analyst Robert Johnson maintains that light and darkness must balance each other in any system.[12] Every creative act needs its opposite. Each building up requires a breaking down. More light will yield more darkness. One cannot exist without the other.

For every extraordinary technological and architectural creation, there is a dark side—more electricity, more greenhouse gasses; more nuclear weaponry, more radioactive storage. What did we have to destroy—how many trees did we cut down, what did we mine from the earth, what fuel sources did we extract—in order to create; and what will we continue to destroy in order to maintain that creation? How can we attend to the dark side, as we nurture the light, so that it won't get the better of us, so that it won't come back to haunt us through ozone holes and pollution?

On an individual level, Johnson suggests practicing ritual or maintenance activities to honor our own darkness—clean house, wash dishes, balance the checkbook, bake bread—anything routine and even tedious, to keep our darkness in check. The principle is simple. If we weed regularly, the weeds won't take over the garden.

I find this an extremely potent lesson and I frame it ecologically for myself. Too many times, I struggle through the dark days that follow the creative ones. Now I practice doing "green" housekeeping chores, embracing the glamourless work I'd like to avoid, to balance my creativity and maintain my emotional health: I pick up trash in the woods, choose ecologically sound products, putter in my garden. I help maintain the system that maintains me.

It is important to recognize that light and dark exist in equilibrium, because the more we attend to the darkness, the more we can bring in the light. The lesson of the balance of day and night, repeated each day, is one of the essential teachings of Genesis.

Since the environmental crisis is a spiritual crisis, a sign of our separation from nature and our selves, we must mend the division and fix the brokenness at the root. We need to practice new ways of knowing, new ways of experiencing nature, new habits, and new values.

A biblical environmental ethic, a creation ethic, is not so much a program of action as it is a sensibility, a kind of knowing, that recognizes the essential mystery in all of life.

Achieving this sensibility requires practice. We can begin by cultivating a kind of "deep seeing," seeing by the light of the soul. Deep seeing means engaging all of our senses to experience the natural world more fully. It involves cultivating an intimacy with the earth. In the language of Martin Buber, it means developing an "I-thou" relationship with nature, rather than an "I-it" one. It means approaching nature as friend.

There's no need to go to the wilderness to develop this friendship. We can do it each time we venture outdoors. Deep seeing means appreciating not only what we think is pretty or nice, but recognizing the beauty or value in all creatures. We can expand our sense of the beautiful by extending our curiosity to the all that appears ordinary.

Deep seeing means appreciating the worms and the bacteria as well as the giraffes and the panda bears; the weeds and the wildness as well as the perennial garden. It means acknowledging both the darkness and the light. All is purposeful in the great work of creation. Jewish philosopher Abraham Joshua Heschel called the experience of deep seeing "radical amazement." When we see with the soul, the ordinary world comes alive with magic and surprises. We see it for what it really is, a place of wonder, and a manifestation of the Divine to be honored and treasured.

2

A I R

THE SECOND DAY

And God said, "Let there be an
expanse in the midst of the water
and let it divide water from water."

And God made the expanse and divided
the water which was below the expanse
from the water which was above
the expanse. And it was so.

And God called the expanse "Heaven!"
And there was evening and
there was morning, a second day.

❧

And God said, "Let there be an **expanse** in the midst of the water
and let it divide water from water."[1] (1.6)

*Va-yomer Elohim yehi **rakia** betokh ha-mayim
vi-yehi mavdil bain mayim la-mayim.*

❧

THE MYSTERY OF AIR

Various Bible commentators have considered the exact meaning of
the creation of the second day, the *rakia*. Many Bibles translate *rakia*
as "firmament" and diagram it as dome-shaped, but no one seems
to really know what it is.

Some rabbis suggested that *rakia* meant a "thinning out of matter." If matter were sufficiently hammered down and flattened out,
you would arrive at its invisible nature.

Others were intrigued with the spiritual aspect of the *rakia*.
Ezekiel said that the *rakia* was formed by the outstretched wings of
the cherubim; it was the throne that God sat on.[2] And Nachmanides
said that *rakia* was so mysterious that we should never mention it.

Rabbi Ibn Ezra proposed that *rakia* means "that which spreads
out" and referred to the "gaseous expanse of the atmosphere," in
other words "air."[3] Given that air is composed of molecules that are
constantly swimming around, reaching beyond, diffusing outwards,
air is a fitting translation of *rakia*. Modern commentators translate
rakia as expanse or space, the container for air. Interpreting *rakia* as
air helps to make ecologic sense of the second day.

Air is invisible, so we tend to take it for granted, but it is a profound and essential creation. Even though it appears as no-thing, it
is a most miraculous some-thing.

According to the laws of chemistry, nitrogen and oxygen, air's
two primary components, should have combined to form nitrates
long ago, but instead they remain free and unbound, allowing us and
all the other creatures to breath. Remarkable too is the perfect bal-

ance of the elements that compose the air. Four percent more oxygen and the whole vegetative world would be consumed in fire.[4]

The *rakia's* physical effects are no less impressive. It is layered, as the rabbis imagined: troposphere, stratosphere, mesosphere, and exosphere, and it acts like a blanket to protect the earth. The stratospheric layer with its component ozone shields the earth and its inhabitants from the sun's potentially deadly ultraviolet radiation, while letting through just the right wavelengths of light necessary for photosynthesis and other essential life processes.

For 3.5 billion years, the earth's atmospheric envelope has maintained an environment that has been hospitable to life and remarkably constant. Without the *rakia*, the world could not stay warm, and the oceans would freeze. The earth would be barren and uninhabitable, scorched like Mercury, whose atmosphere has boiled away, corroded like Venus, where sulfuric acid falls like rain, or frigid like Uranus and Neptune.[5]

Because the *rakia* can travel far and can hold water, the earth enjoys a multitude of climates and all kinds of weather. Around the earth's middle are the doldrums, a belt of constant low pressure and calm waters that give rise to copious rains. North and south of the equator blow the gentle, moisture-laden trade winds that sustain the rainforests. Beyond these, the horse latitudes, named for the stagnant air that slowed ships and forced early explorers to save water by throwing horses overboard, give rise to the deserts. Above and below 35 degrees latitude, where most of us live, the westerlies prevail, creating the wild and unpredictable weather that we call "temperate."

Air is ceaselessly on the move, flowing around the earth and inside our bodies. It breezes through our hair and deep into our lungs. It blows in through our noses, down our windpipes, curving, swirling around through the branches of our pulmonary trees, into the infinite folds of our bronchioles, finally to our alveoli, there dissolving into our blood and carried by our hemoglobin to our hearts and our brains and every cell of our bodies. Because of air, we can think and move and feel.

I have my own internal weather system. When I feel stale and dead inside, suffering my own doldrums, I get on my bike and try to catch some wind. Getting up some speed, I feel the air rushing round my face and whirling through my insides—I hear it whoosh past. The air finds its way into the darkest caverns of my mind and heart. It airs me out and I am revitalized.

I have always been moved by the air. Upon graduating high school my immediate goal was to live outdoors and enjoy the simple pleasure of being exposed to the winds. I wanted to know nature in all of its moods—the crisp, golden days of autumn, the gentle breezes of spring, and the ominous thunderstorms of summer. So I adopted a kind of a Thoreau-inspired life and took to the woods with nothing. I camped out in the Redwood Grove at the edge of Santa Cruz Garden Project, and worked from sunup to sundown in the most remarkable flower garden, living a life inspired by air. Writer Lyall Watson articulated a love of air better than anyone I know when he wrote, "The net result of being in the wind, of being wind-sensitive, is that you end up feeling involved, as though you have some say in the workings of the world."[6]

After college, I found my way to the mountains again, back to the winds, and guided wilderness river trips for several years. In those days, I believed if I wasn't breathing fresh air day in and day out, I wasn't really living.

Immersing myself in air, I somehow sensed the nearness of God. The ancient Israelites must have felt this way too—they spent forty years in the desert on the ultimate hiking trek, exposed to all kinds of weather. They knew God as the east wind blowing locusts to plague the Egyptians and as the pillar of cloud and fire leading their way in the desert. They called God "Rider of the Clouds" and "Most High."

The weather still provides me with hours of entertainment, even though I now lead a more urban life. I catch a glimpse of air whenever I see a vulture winging its way up and around, spiraling on an invisible funnel. I like to sit on my front porch, be still and bear witness to the winds. I listen intently as they grow in strength, howl, and thrash through the trees. Even better, I love to go down to the woods during a storm. All around me, I can feel the energy kick up, and my spirit lifts and soars.

I used to dismiss conversations about weather as small talk. Not anymore. When I take time to notice the wind and clouds and rain, I have a subtle sense of God's presence, streaming inside me and flowing all around me.

❧

And God made the expanse and **divided** the water
which was below the expanse
from the water which was above the expanse. And it was so. (1.7)

Va-ya'as Elohim et-ha-rakia va-**yavdail** bain ha-mayim
asher mi-tachat la-rakia
u-vain ha-mayim asher mai-al la-rakia. Va-yehi khain.

❧

THE BEAUTY OF LIMITS

The idea of setting limits is a critical one in the creation story. God creates by making boundaries.

The original chaos contained everything that was necessary for the making of a universe. The actual work of creation began when God "divided," *yavdail*, the chaos, separating the elements from each other, so that each has a distinct identity and purpose. Dividing, setting limits, is God's modus operandi in the first four days of creation. With a boundary, God made the sky and the sea, created day and night, and formed earth out of water. By establishing limits, God made something extraordinary out of confusion and turmoil.

Limiting one thing makes way for something else. Artists know this. They use boundaries to create. They divide up the world with lines to create space and shapes. Biologists also know this. A cell membrane is a container that holds together what's inside the cell while warding away what's outside; our skin is a sac that holds all our organs and fluids in and keeps harm out. Boundaries provide integrity and protection to that which is bounded off.

The whole earth and all of its variety operate according to strict boundaries. This is the law of the universe. Nature prefers to use just a few patterns over and over, rather than developing millions of new forms to meet each new situation. Spirals, for example, appear in DNA, fiddleheads, abalone shells, fingerprints, stellar galaxies, tornadoes, and whirlpools. Branching patterns appear in trees, plants, pulmonary trees, arteries, and rivers. These patterns limit certain possibilities and expand others. They bring harmony and beauty into the world.

All creatures are bound by their anatomy. The structure of a leg determines if an animal can jump or run or climb or dig. The structure of a beak decides whether a bird will eat worms or seeds or flies. The structure of a tooth determines if a mammal eats flesh or grasses. Freedom comes when structures are used to the fullest, according to their purpose.

Most creatures are also bound by their environment. A species' niche is in part determined by its anatomy. The niche is the creature's ideal habitat, the place where it finds just the right combination of conditions for its unique lifestyle: the foods it likes, the shelter it needs, the proper temperature, the right type of earth, and the specific amount of light and moisture. While the niche provides its creatures with a certain degree of freedom, it also sets limits on the creature's activity. "Fish got to swim and birds got to fly . . ."

In general, violating the limits of anatomy or niche leads a creature to its death. But not for humans. We don't allow the limits of our bodies or our habitats to define our lives. Unique among the creatures, we can change our environment. We don't have a unique niche because, either naturally or with the help of technology, we can occupy almost every niche. Whereas other life-forms are limited to certain bioregions, we can establish ourselves virtually anywhere on earth and beyond, from the ocean depths to the Arctic to outer space. There's nowhere we won't go.

We balk at the idea of limits, both those imposed from without and those imposed by our biology. We thrive on a sense that we can overcome all limits, and we feel triumphant each time we surmount one more boundary. Our pioneering spirit, our desire for conquest, our need to explore the ends of the earth and beyond, our hunger to acquire more and more, our intoxication with unrestrained economic growth—these values have defined our species for millennia.

But each of these boundary-crossings also yields repercussions on the habitats of the earth and the creatures that live there. The atmosphere, the *rakia*, has always borne the consequences of our excesses. The air is a global commons; it is free for the taking; there are no restrictions on its use. But because of its invisible "no-thing" nature, people ignore its life and transgress its boundaries, using it as a receptacle for burnt waste. Through centuries of abuse, the air has become depleted, degraded, congested, and sickened. (In the 1960s, some people even admired air pollution, believing it to be a sign of progress—the symbol of the riches of the developed world.)

Not only does the atmosphere suffer from our exploits; so do we; so do all creatures, because we are all bound by the cyclical nature of the earth. The earth cycles around the sun, water cycles from the oceans to the atmosphere and back down again as rain. Plants absorb carbon from the air during photosynthesis and cycle it back into the atmosphere during respiration. It's all one grand round.

We tend to forget that the earth is round and that whatever we put into the atmosphere naturally circles back to us. We may not feel the effects of our own boundary-crossings, but we all experience the effects of society's collective transgressions. Asthma, skin cancers, holes in the ozone, acid rain, and global warming are evidence of our continual excesses and our invasion into the territory of others.

It is difficult to appreciate the extent to which our society's overindulgence disturbs the processes of life on the earth. The problem is so vast that it is almost incomprehensible. E. O. Wilson compares modern civilization, which has unwittingly extinguished so many of nature's species, with the glaciers that snuffed out all life and terminated the Mesozoic Era some sixty-five million years ago.[7]

✦

Because we are not bound by the limits of our anatomy or the limits of our habitat, humanity's fundamental challenge is to derive its own set of limits and ethics. This is the charge of religion. The Bible is really a manual of stories, laws, and rituals designed to teach humanity the power of limits.

In the beginning, Adam and Eve are gravely punished for the simple act of eating the one fruit that was off limits to them. For one seemingly innocent boundary-crossing, they were alienated from nature forever. But such trespasses are never innocent. To a human-centered eye, crossing the boundary may appear harmless, but from a God-centered perspective the trespass is an invasion of sacred property.

Most of us are not really that much different than Adam and Eve. Our habitual boundary-crossings lead to the destruction of nature and to a loss of identity. We exceed our natural boundaries whenever we look outside ourselves for some "thing" (ultimately of nature) to fulfill a deep inner yearning for love or affection. When we habitually extend beyond our edges, taking more than we need from nature, we lose our balance and a sense of our selves; we mar our own integrity. Our real needs for love, connection, and recognition remain unfulfilled, because we can't satisfy our heart's desire with "things." We grow estranged from our own authentic needs and our deepest selves.

The practice of limiting our selves and honoring the boundaries of others is integral to a creation ethic. Curbing addictions, quitting smoking, avoiding sweets, and refraining from self-destructive behaviors are all self-imposed restrictions that yield greater freedom. So too, reining in the addictive behaviors of taking wantonly from nature.

It's time to find the beauty and pleasures of living within nature's limits. We must limit our consumption to a rate that does not outpace nature's ability to regenerate. We must participate in nature's cycle, taking care that the wastes we create can be integrated back into the circle of life.

❧

And God called the expanse: "**Heaven**!"
And there was evening and there was morning, a second day. (1.8)

Va-yikra Elohim la-rakia **shamayim**.
Va-yehi-erev va-yehi-voker yom shaini.

❧

THE BREATH OF AWARENESS

While the word *rakia*, air, generally connotes the physical nature of the atmosphere, the name *shamayim*, heavens, suggests a more mystical aspect. *Shamayim* is composed of the words *aish*, fire, and *mayim*, water. The fire (light) that is created on day one mixes with the primordial water to form the heavens on day two.

Mystically speaking, the element "air" symbolizes thought or mind. Air is the source of life and consciousness. When God breathed the breath of awareness into a lump of clay, the *adam* became a living being.

The nature of air is to move quickly, to spread far and wide, to travel the world. You can visualize this if you think of boiling water. As you heat water, you give it more energy—the molecules move faster and faster until they evaporate from the water, transforming into vapor, diffusing out in the air. Like air, the mind is on the move, reaching out, exploring, gathering information, learning new things.

Air is the element of communication. Animals know if the world is a threatening place or a safe one by sniffing the air, in search of scents from friend and foe. Our words, the manifestations of our thoughts, are made of exhaled air. So are our songs and our laughter. The Navajo say that we transform the air when we speak, so every utterance actually affects our environment.[8]

Various schools of mystics and thinkers including the alchemists, astrologers, kabbalists, and Jungians understood that we are made up of various combinations of the four elements—air, water, earth, and fire. The elements correspond to the kabbalist's conception of the four levels of the soul: Fire corresponds to *atzilut*/spirit; air corresponds to *briyah*/thought; water corresponds to *yetzirah*/emotion, and earth corresponds to *assiyah*/action.⁹ A healthy life is one that balances all four.

I imagine that I am made mostly of "air," that I live in the world of *briyah*. Some days I am light and breezy, energized by the ideas, connections, revelations that invigorate my mind. Others, I am gusty and piercing, critical and judgmental. Too much mind untamed by the other elements—earth/body, water/heart, and fire/soul—leads to too much willfulness and a need to control the world and ourselves. Jung says that this overabundance of air is particularly characteristic of our age.

Our thoughts and ideas are not necessarily our own; we usually do not just create them. They tend to enter our mind uninvited. They often come from the cultural milieu, from the mythic unconscious, and from God. Ideas can enrich our lives or they can trap us; they can bind us or they can free us. We have to clarify which ones come from a soulful place deep within or a transcendent place without, and which are merely the popular ideas that dominate the world.

The saying goes, "The ideas we have that we don't know we have, have us." We are engulfed by the attitudes of our culture that more is better, that our status is an indicator of our worth, that doing is preferable to being—beliefs that are sometimes anti-ecological, anti-life. Many times we don't even see how these societal attitudes mold us until we are sick or in crisis. It's important to break the spell of these cultural constructs and pay attention to the ideas that move our souls.

"Choose life," the Bible's imperative, is a directive, in part, to choose the ideas by which we live. From time to time I take an inventory of my life to see what I'm choosing and what's choosing me. Am I choosing my friends or did they choose me; am I doing the "right" work; am I following my desires? Or am I responding to some "shoulds" outside of me?

Hopes and dreams are also made of air; they drift into our consciousness like gentle breezes. We are not encouraged to pay attention to them. Suzi Gablik says in her book *The Reenchantment of Art* that we often make fun of hope and optimism and consider such attitudes hokey and pollyannish. In academia, cynicism and negativity are more fashionable than hope and creativity. In environmental circles, laundry lists of troubles are asserted more often than stories of hope. But we need our hopes and dreams to feed our souls—they motivate us to find our true place in the world. They strengthen us and help insure that we don't get sidetracked into living a life of someone else's design.

It's hard work to hang onto those dreams. I try to remember that, contrary to popular opinion, life isn't supposed to be simple. My friend Sandi says, "God doesn't say life will be easy, God says—"Go, follow your calling and I will be with you."

It's important to recognize the power of our thoughts, because we project them onto the world. We know from quantum physics that there is no such thing as an objective reality; we each experience our separate realities. We can make the world a bleak place by projecting onto it our negativities and fears and despair, or we can make it an enchanted one by seeking out its wonder and mystery. We see what we want to see; what we know how to see. Our beliefs have real consequences in the world—they inform our actions. We must be careful how we choose them.

Air is the mysterious invisible flow that envelops and provides for us; it feeds our bodies and the body of the world, and it feeds our minds. The connections between our thoughts, the air, and our breath are revealed in many languages. The Hebrew *ruach* and the Greek *psyche* are variously translated as breath, wind, air, and spirit. *Anima* in Latin is the root for air, breath, and soul. God's ecology is established in these essential relationships.

One way to learn to appreciate the air, to calm our minds and to connect with the spark of life in everything, is by paying attention to our breathing. We breathe in and out approximately twenty-five thousand times a day. Each breath is a connection to the rest of the world, to the dinosaurs, to our ancestors, to the orchids, to the coyotes, to all that lives. We all breathe the same air.

Breathing in and breathing out reflects the basic rhythm of life, the rhythm of the ocean, the rhythm of day and night. By closing our eyes and concentrating on the breath, we can change our perception and move from the mundane nature of life to a connection with our souls and the soul of the world.

When I first encountered breathing practices in my yoga classes many years ago, I would get impatient. I wanted to hurry through the breathing exercises so we could get on with the "more important" vigorous physical "asanas." Now I understand that the breathing is an intensive spiritual exercise itself, which can refresh my body and my perspective on life. Now I relish these moments of following my breath into the unexplored regions of my being.

In Judaism, there are specific prayers that engage the breath as a way into the soul. My favorite one begins with the Hebrew words *Elohai neshamah. Elohai* means my God and *neshamah* means both breath and soul. The prayer begins: "My God, the soul/breath you gave to me is pure. You have created it, you have shaped it, and you breathed it into me." In the Hebrew many of the words of this prayer end with the sound of the breath, "ah." When I chant the Hebrew slowly, I feel my breath streaming through the words, and I find my way back into the spaciousness of my soul. From time to time I see that my own breathing can connect me to God's breathing, *ruach Elohim*, and the soul of the world.

WATER, EARTH, AND PLANTS

THE THIRD DAY

And God said, "Let the water under the sky
be gathered together unto one place and let the
dry land appear." And it was so.

And God called the dry land "Earth!"
And God called the gathering together of the waters
"Seas!" And God saw that it was good.

And God said, "Let the earth sprout
sprout(s), grass seed seed(s) and fruit tree
make fruit after its kind containing its seed
upon the earth." And it was so.

And the earth brought forth sprout(s),
grass seeding seed after its kind and tree making
fruit with seed in it after its kind.
And God saw that it was good.

And there was evening and
there was morning, a third day.

❧

And God said, "Let the **water** under the sky be gathered together unto one place and let the dry land appear." And it was so. (1.9)

*Va-yomer Elohim yikavu ha-**mayim** mi-tachat ha-shamayim el-makom echad ve-tairaeh ha-yabashah. Va-yehi-khain.*

❧

THE SOUL OF WATER

Whereas light is created on day one and air is created on the second day, the third day witnesses the perfection of water and the creation of earth and plants. It is a busy day for God.

The four elements—fire, air, water, and earth, which, according to the ancient Greeks and the kabbalists, were the building blocks for all life—are set forth in the first two-and-a-half days of creation, laying the infrastructure for all that is to come.

The element water is no less miraculous than air or light (fire). Its physical form is remarkable, changing easily liquid to gas to solid. Water can absorb energy and transform it. Able to soak up a tremendous amount of heat, it is an ideal regulator of temperature. Just as water in the blood keeps our cells and organs from overheating, water in seas and lakes can keep the atmosphere from overheating, which is why communities near large bodies of water experience less temperature change than inland areas.

Comprised of nearly 80 percent water, earth is a "water planet." For the 20 percent that is land, water determines its character and vegetation. Forests grow where water is abundant, grassland where it is less plentiful, and deserts where it is driest of all.

Water is the circulatory system of the earth. It is the active element, always on the way somewhere, trickling down to the water table of the earth, hurrying towards the sea in rivers, wafting through the atmosphere on currents of air, or falling to the land as rain or dew. The waters of rivers, streams, oceans, lakes, and aquifers and the droplets contained in clouds and rain are all linked. "All the rivers run into the sea, yet the sea is never full," wrote Ecclesiastes. "From where the rivers come, there they return again."[1]

From the perspective of water, all the earth, the plants, and the animals are channels through which water flows en route to the atmosphere or to the seas. Indeed on a summer's day the trees in an acre of woodland transpire 3,500 gallons into the atmosphere.[2] Together, earth, plants, and atmosphere form a single organism in which water streams like living blood.

Composed of two molecules of hydrogen and one of oxygen, water is positively charged on one side and negatively charged on the other, so it naturally bonds with many substances. Water can absorb contaminants; it cleanses and purifies. It can soften, dissolve, or transform the material it touches—over time even rocks are changed by water. Indeed, water shapes the landscape.

In many cultures water is the element of spiritual transformation. Able to dissolve and transform, water has the power to lift us out of the ordinary and into the holy. The point of baptism and the *mikveh*, the Jewish ritual bath, is not to wash away dirt, but to elevate the soul. Similarly, the Jewish blessing for washing before eating asks us to "lift"—not wash—our hands before indulging in the fruits of the earth. "Infinite are You, Source of Blessing, . . . Who . . . commands us to raise up our hands."

Water glides, flows, and caresses. Unlike air, which travels swiftly and changes direction and intensity on a whim, water moves regularly and rhythmically.[3] On its journey down a river, water can repeat the same pattern at the same place, as it does when it circles behind a stone in a stream, or it can flow in rhythmic curves, as it does in wide valleys or steep canyons. It never moves in a straight line. Even in the oceans, which have no banks, a giant current like the Gulf Stream wends its way like a river within an ocean.

When I was a river guide, the most challenging part of my job was "reading" the water. If I did not recognize what was creating a particular wave pattern, I could end up in a hole and flip the raft. The key was distinguishing between shifting waves caused by drops in the channel, and standing, repeating waves caused by rocks.

Holes, the turbulent whitewater, form when water flowing by a rock curls behind it and heads back upstream. The water gets caught in an unending whirlpool: the bigger the rock and the stronger the current, the more voracious the vortex. The biggest holes can eat you alive. Moving waves, on the other hand, signify that the way is free and clear. Set your boat up to catch the tongue and you're in for a safe, thrilling ride.

On one trip, my friend Steve, another guide, got caught up by the rapture of the river and led his boat right into a hole. The rest of the group watched, horrified. The circling waves thrust Steve out of the boat and revolved him round and round like a washing machine. After what seemed like hours of thrashing about—but was probably no more than two or three minutes—Steve stopped fighting, surrendered his will, and simply stuck out his long legs to catch a downstream current. He was out of that hole in a flash.

According to Jewish mysticism, water symbolizes our feelings and our emotions and is known as the world of *yetzirah*. When we remove the blockages and let our hearts open, we can ride the current of life and we flow. We overflow. "My cup runneth over," wrote the psalmist. But if we're not paying attention and try too hard to control the river, we can end up caught up in our internal backwaters, churning about, lost and exhausted.

Staying in touch with the free-flowing current of our hearts is a challenge. Rabbi Nachman, the eighteenth-century Jewish master, said that finding true joy is the hardest of all spiritual tasks. Perhaps this is because joy and pain must balance each other like light and dark. We can't have one without the other. All feelings come from the same liquid place of our being.

If we are afraid to feel pain, then we often protect ourselves from experiences or relationships that cause us suffering. We do this by clenching our muscles to create a kind of body armor. Yet in protecting ourselves from the potential of pain, we also shield ourselves from the possibility of joy.

When we peel off the armor and allow ourselves the full range of our feelings, we have the opportunity to develop more intimate relations not just with people, but also with nature. A relationship with nature can be the source of tremendous pleasure.

But along with the risk of opening up our heart to nature comes the possibility of experiencing the sadness and pain at its destruction. I can't return to the once tangled woods of my childhood, because I would have to confront their abscence and the absence of the frogs and salamanders that were once abundant in my youthful world. It's not just the loss of these creatures and the loss of my connection to the place that haunts me. It's that I must also acknowledge the underlying causes of their absence: I don't want to face the reality of pollution, sprawl, and climate change, which has taken its toll on the amphibians; it is frightening and overwhelming. "If we look too closely or feel too deeply," writes Terry Tempest Williams, "there may be no end to our suffering."[4]

When experiencing our feelings seems too painful, we often adopt a more intellectual approach to the world, and in so doing, we cut our hearts off from our minds. By choosing a detached, disembodied way of being, we withhold our love, evading the sometimes difficult consequences of loving. We imagine that the heart can't be broken if we don't give it away.

Rabbi Nachman taught that a broken heart is the doorway to our feelings. We should not avoid the experience of a broken heart, because it is our very brokenness that will expand our compassion and our humanity. The more vulnerable we are, the softer our hearts, the more fluid, the more love and joy in our lives and the deeper our relationships with all creatures and all of life.

✒

And God called the dry land **"Earth!"** and God called the gathering together of the waters "Seas!" And God saw that it was good. (1.10)

*Va-yikra Elohim la-yabashah **eretz** u-le-mikvaih
ha-mayim kara yamim. Va-yar Elohim ki-tov.*

✒

THE SOUL OF EARTH

Water and earth are opposites, wrote Samson Raphael Hirsch: *eretz*, earth, is rigid and dry, and *mayim*, water, is liquid and wet.[5] The element earth, or "dry land" as it is first described, has its own mysterious nature. Because land is heavier than water, one would assume that it would sink below the seas when it was created. Noting this, the thirteenth century Jewish mystic and physician Nachmanides claimed that the earth's very existence was positive proof of the existence of God.[6]

The order of the creation corresponds to the sequence of evolution, with land emerging out of water. When the land first appeared, it arose from the sea as one enormous landmass, spanning a quarter of the earth's surface. Over millions of years, the prehistoric landmass, named Pangaea, was pulled apart by earthquakes, forming the continents.

Where water is the element of fluidity and transformation, earth is the element of stability and permanence. Its molecules are fixed in specific patterns, so it remains still, until something acts upon it. The natural forms of the landscape are a testament to the varying degrees of hardness of the earth's minerals and the effects of wind and water on them. Mountains are made of resistant granites, highlands are formed of less resistant marbles, and valleys are shaped from sandstone, the most yielding of all.

Earth has substance, texture, and solidity: it can exist as stone, clay, sand, loam, and mud. It comes in a variety of colors, from deep reds and pinks to dark brown and white. Earth's upper layer, its soil, changes depending on its location: its altitude, latitude, proximity to water, mineral substrate, and the vegetation that grows upon it. Earth is simultaneously mineral, vegetable, animal, and microbial; it is inorganic and organic. It is permeated with air and water. It is in a perpetual process of living and decay, of breaking down and building up. A teaspoon of living earth contains five million bacteria, twenty million fungi, one million protozoa, and two hundred thousand algae.

A sense of the presence of God, an aliveness, permeates the earth, just as it infuses the flow of water, the breath of air, and the light of fire. In the Bible, God is called "Rock," and the earth is considered sacred. God reminds Moses of this, saying, "Remove your sandals because the place on which you are standing is holy ground."[7] Even one of God's names, *Makom*, has the earthy meaning of "place."

The idea that land is the mother of all, continuously bringing forth life, is a testament to the aliveness of the earth. In the Hebrew imagination, the land even expresses feelings: it "mourns," "vomits out," "rejoices," and "is glad."[8] A living being itself, the land was never meant to be a "thing" that could be possessed, plundered, or looted by people.[9] "And the land shall not be sold in perpetuity, for the land is mine; for you are strangers and settlers with me."[10] Human beings were considered sojourners on the earth, which would abide forever.

According to many of the mystical traditions and the four element theory of the ancient Greeks in which all life is understood as a combination of the elements: earth, water, air, and fire, "earth" corresponds to the body, the senses, desire, and our relationships. If we have an overabundance of earth, we may find ourselves reveling too long in the garden of earthly delights. If we lack earth, we may lose touch with our bodies and the body of the world. Earth symbolizes strength, protection, and security. The "salt of the earth" are the humble folk who use their bodies to work hard for a living. Compared to the other elements, earth is sometimes denigrated in our culture. Blue collar laborers, child-care workers, teachers, and mothers, engaged in earth-bound activities, often do not receive the respect they deserve.

Earth is the element that grounds us, gives us backbone, and keeps us strong in the face of adversity. Even though I enjoy earthy activities like puttering in my garden and climbing mountains, there is nothing earthy about me; I lack a strong protective shell. And it's a problem. Without "earth" we are defenseless and tend to over-compensate for our lack of natural strength if we feel threatened. When I have to take a public stand or when I fear people need something from me, I unconsciously tense up and shut down—my friend Mikki says I get "prickly," like a porcupine.

When I'm sick I develop a strange appetite for "earth": I crave beets, turnips, or carrot juice—root vegetables—or liver. I relish these foods, which I usually don't eat, knowing this is nature's way of taking care of me, balancing out my elements. My acupunturist confirms my theory and treats my "earth deficiency" with a potion that tastes like it comes from some dark, musty, place deep underground. I usually don't mind these short bouts of dis-ease, because they give me the opportunity to tune in to nature's magic and my own elemental nature.

In Jewish mysticism, "earth" corresponds to the world of *assiyah*, or action. Earth calls us to turn all of desires and dreams into tangible actions and behaviors.

Sentiment without action is the ruin of the soul. On the other hand, action, devoid of the stories and feelings that can give our actions meaning, may not have the power to sustain our interest and keep us engaged, or may be downright destructive. Too often we reduce environmentalism to just "doing"—to recycling cans or voting for a political candidate who advocates for the environment. While these activities are necessary, such pigeonholing trivializes the earth and all its complexity and diminishes the infinite number of ways we can consciously incorporate a reverence for life and nature into our lives. Equating environmentalism to a few prescribed activities is like equating the Bible with the Ten Commandments or American history with the Declaration of Independence. Without context and depth, environmentalism becomes a meaningless chore.

It's vital to integrate our "fiery" spirit, "watery" feelings, and "airy" thoughts into a "grounded" lifestyle that is meaningful and reflects our innermost being. To walk our talk. We need to find our own stories and relationships with nature that will continually engage us in an ecologically soulful life.

We are all citizens of the earth; we are all bound up in the web of life and we must live out this deep connection. Opening our senses to the pleasures of life, exploring in the great outdoors, finding work that honors nature, living in communities where nature is an integral part, setting ecological standards for our institutions and businesses, choosing natural medicines and wholesome foods that bring us into contact with the earth, and teaching and advocating on behalf of nature all are activities that engage us in the enjoyment of life and the holy repair of the earth.

THE GOODNESS OF WATER, EARTH, AND AIR

The process of "gathering together the waters" and separating out dry land does not stop with the original creation; it continues every day. Rain and snow seep into the earth and are gathered by streams that run to the rivers and finally to the seas. Underwater volcanoes erupt and islands emerge in the midst of oceans. Sandbars are formed as rivers scoop out earth from their outer banks and drop the sediments further downstream. Somewhere erosion breaks down; elsewhere soil builds up. Creation happens everyday, the Jewish prayer book reminds us. "Day by day, in Your goodness, You renew creation."

The proclamation of "goodness" appears twice on the third day—first after water and earth are created, and again after plants are created—and not at all on the second day, when the air was formed and the waters were divided. Since the creations of every other day were deemed "good," commentators have wondered why air was not, and why, water, of all creations, takes two days to make. "Goodness" doesn't come until the middle of the third day when air, water, and earth, all together, are complete.

From an ecological perspective it makes sense that the declaration of "goodness" accompanies the completion of all three elements. The three elements—air, water, and earth—act as a whole. They depend upon each other. Water erodes rock and forms soil. Earth is suffused with water and air. Wind sculpts landscapes. In living systems, none of these elements can exist alone.

The concept of interdependence is fundamental to ecology. Nothing in nature exists as an island, independent of others. The earth can be understood as one living body. In 1785, James Hutton, the father of geology, recognizing that nutrients were recycled through the soil, stated that the earth was one immense super organism and its proper study should be physiology.[11] The soil, which appears so solid and immovable, is in fact part of a larger dynamic interactive system. Seventy-five percent of the entire earth's surface is made of sediments that have been transported by water from one location to another.[12] The Mississippi Delta, for example, is a network of sandbars created by the soils washed downstream from the river's banks and dumped at the entrance to the Gulf of Mexico.

Rachel Carson first popularized the concept of interdependence and pointed out the vulnerabilities of such a dynamic system in 1962 in her book *Silent Spring,* where she produced evidence that pesticides were poisoning waters thirty miles upstream from where they were sprayed. "In the entire water pollution problem," she wrote, "there is probably nothing more disturbing than the threat of widespread contamination of groundwater. It is not possible to add pesticides to water anywhere without threatening the purity of water everywhere."[13] It is not possible to add pesticides to the water without threatening the earth and air as well.

✦

꙳

And God said, "Let the **earth sprout sprout(s), grass seed seed(s)**
and **fruit tree make fruit** after its kind
containing its seed upon the earth." And it was so. (1.11)

Va-yomer Elohim **tadshai** *ha-***aretz deshe aisev mazriya zera**
aitz peri oseh peri *le-mino*
asher zaro-bo al ha-aretz. Va-yehi-khain.

꙳

THE POWER OF SEEDS: DIVERSITY AND SUSTAINABILITY

The third day differs from the first two in the process of creation.
On the first two days, God is the sole Creator. On the third day,
God enlists the earth/*aretz* as a partner: "Let the earth sprout
sprout(s)." Nachmanides points out that the Hebrew word for earth,
aretz, suggests a force that causes growth.[14] The earth has the ability
to grow the creatures that will inhabit it. It is prolific. It is alive.

The earth gives rise to *deshe*, sprouts, anything that shoots
from the ground, including bacteria, fungi, and moss as well as
"seed-bearing" plants: grasses and fruit trees.[15] It is noteworthy that
God calls forth all kinds of diverse plants and not just edible ones
that people can eat. In this regard the Bible is markedly ecological
and biocentric. Compare the biblical story to the Babylonian creation myth in which the god Marduk creates just one type of
plant—vegetables for human consumption.

With the earth's sprouting sprouts, the biblical order of creation again coincides with the evolutionary sequence. Two types of
deshe or sprouts, bacteria and fungi, prepared the earth for the flowering of the world. Bacteria are, in scientist Lynn Margulies words,
"metabolically gifted:" they thrived where no others could, in the
oxygen-free environment of the early earth. Blue-green bacteria
could capture light energy and break water molecules apart. They
combined the hydrogen molecules from the water with the carbon
molecules from the atmospheric CO_2 to build their bodies, while
discarding the unneeded oxygen molecules back into the atmos-

phere. Earth's atmosphere grew oxygen-rich simply by bacteria living their lives.[16] And earth's rocky substrate grew fertile as bacteria and fungi turned stone into soil. An oxygen-rich environment and a loamy fertile ground paved the way for the evolution of green seed-bearing plants (*aisev*/grasses and *aitz peri*/fruit trees).

The essential creation of the third day is seed-bearing plants. The word seed, *zerah* (in one form or another), appears six times in verses 11 and 12, yet nowhere are leaves, stems, bark, or flowers mentioned. Rather plants are only discussed in terms of their seeds, the product of plant sex.[17] Grass must "seed seeds" and fruit trees must "make fruit with seed." Sex—plant sex anyway—is a biblical imperative just as it is an ecological one.

Grasses, *aisev*, and fruit trees, *aitz peri*, are two of the earth's primary types of seed-bearers. Grasses make up most of the herbaceous plants and give us all of our grains; they cover fully one third of the land surface of the earth and can be found at the edges of climactic extremes where no other plants survive. Grasses like wheat, rye, rice, corn, oats, barley, sorghum, and millet are the staple food for the animals and people who inhabit their lands.

Fruit trees provide sweet and immediate foods that animals and people can eat right off the branch: no heating, soaking, or baking required.[18] Ecologically speaking, fruit trees also provide shade for cooling the earth and its creatures, and habitat for a host of insects and animals. Their roots hold the soil in place and their leaves build the soil. Trees also play a critical role in the global ecology, replenishing the oxygen supply, purifying the air, and regulating temperature.

The seed-bearers were wildly successful because of their unique ability to literally catch light-waves (photons) and make food for themselves and everyone else. With no means of movement of their own, green plants were able to exploit environments around the world because their seeds travel freely in the guts or fur or feathers of other creatures, or on the wind.[19]

In its emphasis on seeds, the Bible is offering a profound ecological message about the necessity of sustainability. The repeated phrase "after its kind" underscores this message. From the perspective of survival and continuity, seeds are the most significant part of the plant.[20] Seeds are the secret to a plant's ability to populate the earth and continue its family line in perpetuity. Even Nachmanides noted: "[God] decreed that there be among the products of the earth a force which grows and bears seed so that the species should exist forever."[21]

Because of seeds, corn will not bear apples or potatoes; corn will only make corn. Seeds encode the law of the species, the possibilities and limits.[22] Seed plants hold the key to sustainability.

While seeds guarantee sustainability, they also promise diversity and change. Seeds result when two individuals from the same species come together to produce a totally unique being; the offspring's shape, size, color—all of its features—are different from its parents. If a species is to survive in a variety of conditions: wet/dry, hot/cold, acid/alkaline, then sex is a perfect way to diversify the species and create individuals who may happen to have just the right set of characteristics to adapt to a new situation.

We can't fully appreciate the marvel of sex unless we consider its alternative: asexual reproduction. An amoeba, for example, simply splits in half when it gets too big, forming an identical replica of its parent. An asexual species can live happily ever after into the future, just as long as its environment remains constant. No sex means no diversity and no change and no possibility for the species to survive if its environment changes.

Seeds promise diversity, and through diversity, evolution happens; possibilities emerge. God's prescription for seeds on the third day is a prescription for biological diversity and a hopeful future.

LIMITING THE POTENTIAL OF SEEDS: MONOCULTURE

Nature loves diversity. In nature, many different kinds of plants grow together in symbiotic communities. Rarely do you find a single species of wild plant growing in dense concentrations by itself. This mix of plants is the primary reason that plant communities can sustain themselves. In the long run a community can overcome the vagaries of wind, weather, and a host of environmentally adverse conditions, while an individual species cannot.

In contrast to the diverse, sustainable communities that occur in nature, modern agriculture cultivates monocultures in which single species of annual plants are raised in dense concentrations for acres on end. Corn is grown in one area, wheat in another, soybeans in another, and so on. Monocultures clearly have production and economic benefits. It's easier and more efficient to plant, cultivate, care for, and harvest one type of plant in one place than to have many crops with different requirements all mingled together.

But monocultures face a host of problems. A field of one identical species grown in monoculture is easy prey for pathogens. With no variant species to hinder the pest, the pathogens get stronger and multiply faster. Bacteria can make their way through a whole field, destroying every single plant. When the potato blight struck Ireland in 1845, farmers were growing just two kinds of potatoes. The blight spread quickly, decimating the entire crop because there were no resistant strains to thwart its course. In the Andes, where the blight also hit, there was no disaster because the hundreds of blight-resistant potato relatives, growing among the susceptible strains, were able to survive and reproduce.

Annual crops grown in monocultures also deplete the soil of nutrients and water and require enormous amounts of fertilizer. Annuals species all die back in the fall, exposing the soil to wind, water, and all kinds of weather, and the soil washes or blows away. In the last one hundred years, monoculture farming has led to the loss of 50 percent of our topsoil's latent productivity. In contrast, the native prairie, composed of communities of diverse perennials, keeps on building and improving the soil, sustaining itself and the creatures who graze there.[23]

Today, monoculture farming is the dominant form of agriculture. Like the fashion industry, the agricultural and chemical companies develop sexy new products each year to lure customers. Agribusiness rejects traditional seeds and, instead, develops new hybrids that are large, fast-growing, easy to pick and transport, resistant to disease and drought, and able to withstand a long shelf life.

With the focus on a few easy-to-market hybrids, monoculture farming inevitably has led to decreased species diversity. According to one study, of the over seven thousand kinds of apples that grew in the United States a hundred years ago, 977 varieties exist today.[24] Likewise, only ten varieties of wheat and six of corn make up most of our harvest. The story is the same throughout the world. Fifty years ago in India, farmers grew more than thirty thousand traditional varieties of rice. Now ten kinds account for 75 percent of India's rice crop.[25]

Today the most frightening threat to species diversity and, indeed, to the integrity of seeds are genetically modified crops—plants whose DNA has been reengineered to capitalize on a desired trait of another species. In 1997, farmers planted nineteen million acres of U.S. farmland with genetically modified organisms (GMOs). One year later that number nearly tripled. Worldwide, by 1998, more than half the world's soybeans and one third of the corn came from GMOs.[26] Genetically modified crops pose the same problems of all monocultures, and then some. Insects can't differentiate between genetically modified corn and "natural" varieties. As they travel from plant to plant, they invariably brush pollen from the genetically modified plant onto the reproductive organs of the "natural" plant, thereby altering the integrity of the seeds forever.

Today there is growing concern that the large-scale introduction of transgenic crops could mean the contamination of wild plants and the destruction of our God-given seeds.[27] Who knows what havoc we wreak, what possible futures we deny as we manipulate our seeds, our sacred genetic reservoirs.

᳆

And the earth brought forth sprout(s), grass seeding seed after its kind
and tree making fruit with seed in it after its kind.
And God saw that it was **good**. (1.12)

*Va-totzai ha-aretz deshe aisev mazriya zera liminaihu
ve-aitz oseh peri asher zaro-bo le-minaihu.
Va-yar Elohim ki-**tov**.*

᳆

DIVERSITY: THE PATH TO PARADISE

The Jewish sages said that God created the Garden of Eden—paradise—on the third day.[28] The primary features of Eden are rich, fertile soil, pure, flowing streams, and an incredible variety of trees and greenery: all creations of the third day, all "good."

Paradise, according to the rabbis, was biologically diverse. They said that there were "eighty myriads of trees in every corner of Paradise" and that the "Tree of Life had fifteen thousand tastes and it stood in the middle."[29] Perhaps there was some truth to this rabbinic fantasy. Evan Eisenberg tells us that "Canaan as a whole, situated at the junction of three continents, has always been a maelstrom of gene flow. Even today its genetic diversity is dazzling."[30]

Ezekiel described the Garden of Eden as an ecosystem in perfect health, diverse and harmonious.

> I saw gigantic trees on both banks of the stream. . . . Every living creature that swarms will thrive wherever this stream goes; the fish will be abundant once these waters have reached them . . . and the fish will be of various kinds and most plentiful, like the fish of the great sea. . . . All kinds of trees for food will grow up on both banks of the stream. Their leaves will not whither and their fruits will not fail; they will yield fruit each month.[31]

God's garden is wild and rich, brimming with the most unimaginable variety. Paradise is the expression of God's ecological exuberance.

When I first arrived on the outskirts of Philadelphia on a spring day about twenty years ago, I thought I had entered paradise. The earth was exploding in flowers: azaleas flaunted tropical erotic colors of fuchsia, peach, and scarlet; their cousins, the rhododendrons, paraded giant blossoms of crimson and pink; the mountain laurels rang their elegant pink bells, and the dogwoods stood dignified, draped in graceful white blossoms. Coming from New England and California, where people are proud—even self-righteous—about their landscapes, I had minimal expecta-

tions as to what I would find in Philadelphia. I never imagined I
would be bowled over.

Were Ezekiel to come to eastern Pennsylvania, Penn's Woods,
perhaps he, too, might have thought he had arrived in paradise. The
first European settlers who landed here four hundred years ago described clear, pristine streams; rich, loamy soils; and "all kinds" of
"gigantic" trees, some as large as twenty feet in diameter and two
hundred feet high. Even today with Pennsylvania's invasive plants,
the absence of chestnut trees, and an overabundance of deer, many
trees in Penn's woods are of majestic form—seemingly gigantic—
and the forest itself is altogether diverse. From the dappled piebald-
barked sycamore to towering tulip trees, to the clear, smooth, broad-
bodied beech, to the aromatic sassafras, to the hardy oaks—the
eastern forest is plentiful indeed. Unique to this forest is also a lush
understory of flowering shrubs, including hydrangeas, fragrant cean-
othus, maple leaf viburnum, and blueberry. Together with the diverse
kinds of flowering plants including jack-in-the-pulpit, may apples,
false Solomon's seal, skunk cabbage, foam flower, waxy yellow sun-
drops, cheerful monkey flower, wild ginger, bright orange butterfly
weed, Jacob's ladder, and goldenrod, Penn's Woods is prolific. And as
in Ezekiel's paradise, this forest gives "fruit" in abundance.

Wherever diverse kinds are flourishing together in healthy communities, paradise lives. Paradise need not look like Shangri-La.
Were Ezekiel to have had his vision in the southwest, he might have
described paradise in the way that nature writer Edward Abby did:

> When I write paradise I mean not only apple trees and
> golden women, but also scorpions and tarantulas and flies,
> rattlesnakes and gila monsters, sandstone, volcanoes, and
> earthquakes, bacteria, bear, cactus, yucca, bladderweed,
> ocotillow and mesquite, flashfloods and quicksand and
> yes, disease and death and the rotting of flesh. Paradise is
> the here and now, the actual, tangible dogmatically real
> Earth on which we stand, yes. God Bless America the
> Earth upon which we stand.[32]

PARADISE LOST? MORE MONOCULTURE

Today, the paradisial exuberance of the American Eden has been squelched by our modern predilection for quantity, convenience, and size rather than quality, complexity, and depth. Witness the flowering of the monocultures.

The term "monoculture" is not reserved for agriculture alone. Monocultures result whenever character and soul are traded for practicality and efficiency; when uniformity takes the place of diversity. Most glaringly, monocultures have taken over America's once pastoral countryside.

Today America's rural paradise has been denuded and flattened to make way for monocultures of near-identical, gigantic, single-family homes, otherwise known as McMansions, and nondescript strip malls, decorated largely with the same three kinds of plants. Outside my home of Philadelphia, new development is consuming the open space and farmlands of Bucks County, the landscape that inspired "O What a Beautiful Morning," at the rate of one acre an hour.

The conversion of once diverse woodlands and farmlands into strip malls, highways, and housing developments is known as "sprawl," and the sprawling developments outside the city are called "exurbs." According to several dictionary definitions, sprawl means: to lie with arm and legs spread awkwardly and unnaturally in all directions, to extend over something in an ungainly or ugly way, or to take up more space than is necessary. The designation seems altogether appropriate.

Since the '60s, my home state of Pennsylvania has lost more than four million acres of farmland and woodland to sprawl, an area larger than Connecticut and Rhode Island combined. This is not because our numbers are expanding; in fact, the population of Pennsylvania's cities has decreased in the last fifty years. Yet just outside the cities, home size has increased by 26 percent and land development has increased by 80 percent.

The Pennsylvania Environment Commission says that nothing in the last fifty years has been more harmful to the natural world in terms of air pollution (from traffic), environmental degradation, and global warming, than sprawl. New sprawling developments require new roads. Bulldozers excavate tons of soil, rip out trees, flatten the landscape and reroute streams. Once bucolic, pristine creeks—sickened by muddy, chemical-laden runoff from lawns and blacktop—have become channels for contaminated wastes. And resident species, bereft of their habitat, are forced to leave or die.

Besides violating ecological systems and the integrity of landscapes, sprawl hinders the possibility of community. Even though developers take pains to make the spotless homes and their surroundings look like communities, creating arcadian-type landscapes with mature trees and shrubs, and giving them evocative names like Thornton's Woods, River's Edge, and Pine Grove, these are not real communities by any stretch of the imagination.

Developments often lack the physical design that's needed to bring people together to create community. Most developments have no town centers, no sidewalks, no corner stores, and no place to congregate or walk. They often lack "diverse kinds," particularly people from varying class and economic backgrounds. And they lack soul. Driving around the looping roads of these "communities" there is the haunting sense that one could be anywhere . . . and at the same time nowhere.

The monoculture that typifies sprawl, from the identical homes to the endless roads to the poverty of plant diversity, is clearly at odds with the vision of paradise that Genesis envisions.

Sprawl breaks my heart. The Eden-like woods outside the city where I once went for weekend trips fed my imagination and restored my soul. Up until about ten years ago there were still plenty of small towns and backwoods to discover by bike or foot within an hour of the city. Now with the congested roads and acres of look-alike housing units, there are really very few places outside of the city worth exploring.

I wonder about kids who grow up in sprawling developments. Where do they build their forts and their tree houses and hide-aways? Where do they hunt for pollywogs and butterflies? Where do they go to live out their fantasies? Where do they learn to love the earth?

I wonder what happens to the landscape of the mind when the outer landscape is so flat and predictable. We are all affected by what we see every day. I am sure that the absence of variety and surprise colors our perception and influences the attitude we bring to our culture and to ourselves. Do those who live in look-alike houses think alike? Do they struggle more to keep up with the Joneses? A psychiatrist friend told me that he had a patient, a teenage girl who became bulimic when her family moved from the city to the exurbs; the girl blamed her condition on the pressure to conform and the extreme isolation that she felt in her environment.

Our romance with the exurbs has had profound and detrimental effects on the cities as well. For decades after World War II, the Veterans Administration and the Federal Housing Authority zealously promoted suburbia at the expense of cities, giving preferential ratings and tax breaks to those who would purchase suburban homes. While federal and state governments poured millions of taxpayer dollars into new highways, thereby encouraging the outward migration of residents and industries away from the cities, they neglected to give more money to the public transportation systems upon which cities depend. In addition government agencies developed strict environmental regulations, making it prohibitively expensive for businesses to redevelop older urban industrial sites (they have to pay to clean up the last occupants' toxic wastes) and so they, along with thousands of bright and productive employees, have had to leave the cities to find more affordable environments.

Together these factors have contributed to a trend that fosters the concurrent development of exurbia and the deterioration of the cities. About a half million people have left Philadelphia since World War II, leaving behind more than fifty thousand abandoned homes, three thousand vacant lots, and an increasingly poor population.

Similar stories are told in urban centers across America. According to Thomas Hylton, author of *Save our Lands, Save our Towns:*

> The biggest story of the last fifty years in Pennsylvania, one that should make us ashamed, has been the senseless abandonment of this once magnificent city [Philadelphia], the most historic in America, in order that we could simultaneously destroy some of the most beautiful landscapes and finest farmland in the world.[33]

PARADISE REDISCOVERED

As I sadly witness sprawl encroach on our once pastoral landscapes, I have tried to do something besides bemoan the loss. For a while, I volunteered on a committee at a local lands trust, an organization that helps to preserve green space and plans for smarter development in the exurbs. Lately, I have turned my attention towards the city and my own neighborhood. The redevelopment of urban centers represents the greatest hope for combating sprawl, preserving nature, and improving the quality of life for the greatest number of people.

This attitude reflects a major shift in my own perspective. Many years ago, as a youthful and ideological environmentalist, I thought cities were the bane of humanity, and humanity the bane of nature. I fashioned for myself a life lived simply in the woods, avoiding cities entirely. Luckily, before I grew too miserable and crotchety, I realized that we humans are ourselves an extraordinary part of nature, and while we do have the capability to ruin the world, we also have the opportunity to restore it.

Now I am able to recognize paradise in the flowering of so much cultural diversity in cities. I am interested in how people naturally express their creativity in countless ways: how they enrich their communities, grow their gardens, and cook their foods. On a recent adventure, I went for a drive with a friend through what is often considered the wasteland of north Philadelphia to visit some of the community gardens. There we found innumerable oases of green and beauty—gardens crowded with many kinds of lettuce, unruly squash and pumpkins, tomatoes bursting our of their cages, strawberry patches, chard, beets, potatoes, colorful pink hollyhocks, and royal blue delphinium. Cheerful eight-foot sunflowers stood as proud sentries at the entryway to many of the gardens, inviting passersby to come in and sit for a spell. The gardens afforded the communities more than plots for cultivating plants; they served as a gathering place for conversations, meetings, and barbeques, fostering pride among the gardeners and the neighbors.

Dazzling murals that have cropped up on every available wall in some of the most bereft neighborhoods also speak to the creative impulse that thrives in the city. Drawing on the best of peoples' talents, the murals are a team effort that celebrate the distinct personality of each place.

I am also interested in how individuals make their nests. The row houses that typify the inner city, standing merely fifteen feet wide, have their own virtue. In a world so characterized by conspicuous consumption and greed, there is a certain elegance in a home and a yard that is sized to fit the needs of its inhabitants, and no more. There is a beauty in humility and proportion.

Rather than expressing their individuality in terms of the size of their homes, city dwellers find other ways to express themselves. On one excursion I passed a row house with a large front lot that, at first glance, resembled a junkyard. But when I got closer, I saw a garden of flying horses and whimsical creatures collected from carousels and carnivals from days long forgotten. High above, atop tall poles, the horses were prancing through the air. The garden was rich with found art in every direction.

The city is indeed its own kind of garden, giving rise to both cultural and natural diversity. A wide array of plants grow wild here, though we may not appreciate them because we are so accustomed to a domesticated aesthetic. Sumac, daisies, mullein, milkweed, chicory, and morning glories all flourish in sidewalk cracks, railroad yards, rubble heaps, and abandoned lots. These plants, which we categorize as weeds, don't care whether they grow on a poor man's ground or rich; they still provide all of the same services as a cultivated garden or park: purifying the air, casting shade, and offering green relief to anyone who wants to partake of their gifts.

You're never far from nature in the city: from spring floods to summer drought, from a mud puddle to water from a faucet that originates in an outlying reservoir, from cats and dogs to pigeons and nighthawks and Canada geese, from butterflies and fireflies to cockroaches. Without espousing any kind of political agenda, city living in and of itself embodies the marriage of culture and nature and lays the foundation for a sustainable environmental lifestyle.

The web of community that urban living fosters is another dimension of paradise as I now understand it. My own neighborhood of Mount Airy is rich with a kind of communal integrity woven together by a walking lifestyle. I walk to the co-op, to the synagogue and the woods and friends' homes. Living here, I don't need to plan my social encounters because I run into everyone I want to see as a part of my daily routine. Caring grows because we see each other regularly on the street and are aware of each other's woes and triumphs. It's no effort to shop for a sick neighbor, to make a *shiva* (condolence) call, to pick up a neighbor's child at school—it's all part of the fabric of community life. This type of integrated community living is absent in many exurbs where people live further from their neighbors and need to get in a car and drive to a store just to pick up a quart of milk.

When I feel despair over the loss of paradise and all of its diversity, I do my best to celebrate whatever diversity I can find. The celebration begins at home with the foods that I eat. If I buy vegetables grown by local farmers I can do a small part to keep the neighboring farms and the local color alive. Local farmers often use traditional seeds, "seeds seeded from seeds," rather than genetically manipulated ones, so buying locally achieves several goals simultaneously—it says "no" to agribusiness, genetic engineering, and a certain cultural flatness, and "yes" to the traditional small farm, diversity and the God-given integrity of seeds.

Since most fruits and vegetables are exposed to gasoline fumes and other hazards of the road as they travel approximately thirteen hundred miles across several state borders to reach our tables, it is also much healthier to eat produce grown by local farms. And fresher vegetables are juicer and sweeter. Not to mention that buying locally means fewer trucks on the highway sending noxious gases and smut into the atmosphere.

My neighbor Claudia is doing more than anyone I know to preserve our local farms and farmers. For months she's been going to Lancaster County to meet with Amish farmers to educate them about the finicky tastes of city folks and to learn from them about the difficulties that they encounter every day—the unpredictability of the weather, the cycle of drought, the late frost which killed the broccoli and cabbage crops, the costs of sustaining an organic farm and the challenges of competing in the marketplace. If she can help them market their crops in a viable way, they may not have to sell their family farms to another housing developer. Claudia always comes home loaded with stories and bundles of produce from the farmers who have adopted her. This spring, she gathered together a bunch of neighbors and engaged them in a partnership with one of the local farms as a C.S.A.—Community Supported Agriculture co-op.

C.S.A. members make a commitment to a particular farm at the beginning of the growing season by buying shares in the farm. In return, they receive farm-fresh, locally grown, typically organic produce each week from late spring through early fall. The benefits of this system are countless for farmer and community. The farmer benefits by having a guaranteed income at the beginning of the growing season and the fairest return on the produce. The local community benefits from delicious and healthy foods and increased revenues in the local economy. Everyone benefits from the peace of mind obtained from knowing that they're helping save at least one more family farm from extinction.

In her small C.S.A. in Mount Airy, Claudia tells me that four households of the thirty are rabbinical students from the Reconstructionist Rabbinical College located nearby. I am heartened to hear this. I imagine a tiny army of students infiltrating congregations with a new idea and a new possibility for *tikkun olam*, repair of the earth. When we have a connection to the place where our food comes from and the people who grow it, the simple act of eating becomes a spiritual opportunity and an act of social responsibility. What better program to join head, heart, and hand?

And **there was evening and there was morning,** a third day. (1.13)

Va-yehi-erev va-yehi-voker yom shelishi.

A SENSE OF PLACE

Genesis provides an orderly picture of the universe. The form of the narrative itself is orderly. Each day begins with the words: "And God said" and ends with: "There was evening and morning, a second (third, etc.) day." Order is inscribed in the creation with a set of balanced pairs: heaven and earth, day and night, sky and sea, the waters and dry land. Each element has a definite purpose, place, and day. Philo, the ancient Greek Jewish philosopher, said that the word *tov*, which is usually translated as "good," means orderly, and he translated the recurrent refrain that brings each day to a close, "And God saw it was orderly."[34]

Tuning into the order—the purpose and place—of the creation may inspire us to achieve our own sense of purpose in the world. Ecologically speaking, our purpose is intimately bound with our geographic place. Each creature ultimately belongs to its habitat. Who we are stems, in part, from the place in which we live.

Several years ago a story, the origin of which remains unclear, appeared in Jewish environmental circles. It described two people arguing over the ownership of a piece of land. The dispute was resolved when a passerby suggested that the matter be put to the land itself. He knelt down to ask the land the question, then put his ear to the ground for an answer. He arose and proudly proclaimed: "Gentlemen, the land belongs to neither of you; you belong to it."

The meaning of the tale resonates. We all belong to the land, and the land helps to form us. Getting to know the place that supports us can give us a deeper sense of ourselves. The sense of home is deeply encoded in our psyches. Environmentalists often maintain that having a "sense of place"—a sense of intimacy with the land that sustains us, a familiarity with the streams, the weather, the plants and their habits, the local culture—is an overlooked dimension of an environmental ethic.

William McDonough asks us to consider ourselves "natives" of the places that we inhabit. If we root ourselves in our place, and work, play, and celebrate there, we're more likely to care for that place. When place or nature becomes an abstraction, as it is for many of us, then it's difficult to cultivate a feeling for it. "The man who is often thinking that it is better to be somewhere else than where he is excommunicates himself," writes Thoreau. "To withhold yourself from where you are is to be cut off from communion with the source."[35]

We are called to give ourselves to our place. The call comes to me from my garden. I'm quite sure that one way I can help to fix the world (*tikkun olam*) and myself is to create Eden in the backyard.

I have lived in the same spot in the Wissahickon Valley (within the city limits of Philadelphia) for twenty years now, and every year my little plot of Eden grows more beautiful and diverse. My property is long and narrow like a bowling alley. When I first bought it, the yard consisted of a sparsely planted garden and a long weedy lawn surrounded by overgrown thickets.

My initial plan was to turn the shady section behind the house into a woodland garden. Being cash poor and land rich, I collected plants from my Aunt Doris's renowned formal garden six hours north in Newburyport, Massachusetts. I brought home a carload of plant divisions: ginger, trillium, phlox, Aruncus, Astilbe, and ferns. She presented me with one of her prize Japanese jack-in-the-pulpits, which has since established itself comfortably in my soil.

Once I started collecting, it was hard to stop. I was on the lookout for avid gardeners who needed to divide their plants. I discovered neighbors and made lots of new friends, eager to spread their wealth. Betty, a seventy-five-year-old retired architect, who transformed the sprawling lawn at the Upsal Garden Apartments into a funky garden, gave me bee balm, lambs ears, Lamium, and a Lenten rose. Steve provided a Douglas fir and excavated an ailing azalea from our co-op that needed a new home. My next-door neighbor Liz, an artist and gardener extraordinaire, invited me to dig up her bear's britches, Houtouenia, Echinacea, and Bryonia. Claudia contributed a nice array of unusual daylilies, and Cyd dropped off a Malva and a pea plant. Establishing a garden offered me expression for my artistic nature, and scavenging for plants satisfied all my primal hunting and gathering needs.

When Judd moved in, he set to work on the secret sunny garden in the far back. He drew a circle in the middle, laid out eight diagonals for paths, and established eight ray-like beds in between. My neighbor Brad supplied roofing tiles, perfect for stepping stones, that he had collected from a building demolition downtown. We took our time preparing the beds, and then the planting began.

In the early years of the garden, I was primarily interested in the display of flowers: the deeper the color, the more exotic looking, the better. As my vision expanded and my taste matured, I began to see more than the flowers. I became interested in the leaves: their colors, shapes, and textures, and how they looked in relation to each other, how contrast enhanced their beauty. I began to appreciate hundreds of textures, from the puckered blue leaves of the giant hostas to the fine, feathery ones of Liatris. I noticed what seemed like an infinite array of leaf colors from lime green to silver to deep purple.

I love living a farming life in the city. I visit the plants in the morning to see what's new before venturing off to work. On weekends I attend to all the details: watering, digging, dividing plants, preparing beds, tending compost, and (my favorite) transplanting. When the plants are overgrown or ill suited to their spot—too much light, not enough light, too wet, too dry—I take the time to figure out what's wrong and then find them a new, more suitable home.

I'm not the only gardener here. If I were, I might have abandoned the garden project long ago. I live in, and am helping establish, a gardening culture in my neighborhood. Having a community of gardeners increases the pleasure: we trigger each other's imagination, swap plants, share information, participate in the annual garden tour, and generally inspire each other. We make our gardens for our friends, not just for ourselves. It's communal art and it binds us together.

Having a garden community also increases the possibilities for real *tikkun olam*. Recently, I was introduced to the book *Noah's Garden*. Author Sara Stein has an inspiring idea for our backyards. She recognized that most lawns and gardens, whether city or suburban, reflect a certain kind of poverty, a lack of diverse kinds of species. This indigence in plant species leads in turn to a dearth of animal species (we all have more than enough squirrels and plenty of deer, but that's all we have). Animals, like people, won't live in a place where they can't find a good meal.

So a good steward, who has even an inkling of a vision of "yard as ecosystem," can actually help restore the land.[36] This is particularly good news for the suburbs and the exurbs.

Sara Stein advocates experimenting with a diverse array of native trees and berry-bearing shrubs, which can serve as food for animals, and tall perennials, which can serve as cover for animals. Her ideas are all the more effective when many neighbors share a similar vision, when everyone is planting native trees and shrubs around the perimeter of their properties, creating a greenway throughout the community. Just imagine who will come home to roost.

I love this idea, and I think it will work nicely in my neighborhood as well. My next project will be a Noah's Garden club on my block. Membership in the club consists of simply planting one native shrub on one's property border each year.

✦

Although Genesis teaches us about order and boundaries, this does not imply we are meant to impose some regimented order on the world. We won't find a sense of place by planting marigolds in a row like soldiers. Quite the contrary. The creation story is not about a human created order; it's about the inherent God-given order of nature: its integrity, the rightness of each creation in its place, which to us may seem chaotic. Gardening teaches this; it teaches the art of caring for a place. If you want a good garden, you learn the habits and idiosyncrasies of your plants, you follow their lead, give them the right conditions, and let them be. Over time, you'll find a new connection and responsibility and a feeling of intimacy with the place you call home.

In the beginning, God created the elements, the foundation materials and energies for life: earth, water, air, and fire. And God created seeds and a mechanism for life to replicate itself and diversify forever.

No creation is an island. Each is involved in an infinite number of relations—most unseen. Each is inextricably bound to an ecosystem that is much larger than itself, to the web of life. The ultimate goodness, paradise, comes with the flowering of all of these relations.

The primary creation of the third day is plants. Plants teach us about rootedness and dependency, about diversity and sustainability, and about belonging to a place.

We need to find our own sense of place, a balance of the God-created order and the order we derive ourselves. By rooting ourselves in our local diverse communities, by rehabbing old homes, planting native species, purchasing local products, eating whole foods that maintain genetic integrity, and involving ourselves in neighborhood activities, we can help to create paradise where we live, and avoid ruining the paradise of our rural lands. There's nothing that we can do that will help our earth more than staying put in our cities, villages, towns, and inner-ring suburbs, and cultivating the simple pleasures of walking, talking, living in community, and gardening. We need to make our older neighborhoods "fashionable" again and take pride in them. A creation ethic calls us to invest ourselves in our place.

4

PLANETS AND TIME

THE FOURTH DAY

*And God said, "Let there be lights in the
expanse of the heaven to divide the day from
the night, and let them be for signs and for
seasons and for days and for years."*

*And they will be for lights in the expanse
of the heaven to shine upon the earth.
And it was so.*

*And God made the two great lights,
the greater light to rule the day and the smaller
light to rule the night, and the stars.*

*And God gave them to the expanse of
the heaven to light up the earth*

*and to rule over the day
and over the night and to divide
between the light and the darkness.
And God saw that it was good.*

*And there was evening and
there was morning, a fourth day.*

❧

And God said, "Let there be lights in the expanse of the heaven
to divide the day from the night, and let them be for
signs and for **seasons** and for **days** and for **years.**"[1] (1.14)

*Va-yomer Elohim yehi meorot bi-rekia ha-shamayim
lehavdil bain ha-yom u-vain ha-laylah ve-hayu
le-**otot** u-le-**moadim** u-le-**yamim** ve-**shanim**.*

❧

THE ECOLOGY OF TIME

Each of the creations of the first three days was coupled with its
corresponding creation in the next three days. On the fourth day
God created the light bearers in the sky to capture the light of the
first day and light up the earth.[2] (Similarly, birds and fish of the fifth
day were designed to capture the essence of water and air, and land
animals and humans of the sixth day were designed for the earth.)
The heavenly lights, including the sun, the moon, the stars, and the
planets, act as signs and make time as they cut through the sky, shin-
ing their light.

The rabbis said the luminaries of the sky provide four types of
time-consciousness for those of us who dwell on earth: *otot,
moadim, yamim,* and *shanim. Otot* are "signs," unpredictable events
like eclipses and meteor showers, that occur outside of the regular
cycling of the planets, portending the miraculous. They call us to
wake up to life's wonders and make meaning out of moments.

Moadim are seasons. The round of seasons is nature's clock.
Every season has its own unique qualities of light, scent, taste, and
color. Each calls for particular activities from growth to exuberance
to fullness to quiescence. Each reflects a specific aspect of the life
cycle: birth, development, maturity, and death.

Yamim are days. The days bring to mind a kind of deep time
that began eons ago and stretches on and on into the future and
around again to the beginning—an ocean, *yamim,* of days, *yamim.*

This is eternal time: it goes on forever and our lifetimes make up a mere microsecond of it.

Shanim are years; *shana* also means change. *Shanim* refers to the changes that compose a life. This is linear, measurable time: time on a human scale.

Time has depth and integrity; it is whole and full. It has boundaries, just like space. Genesis reflects a kind of ecology of time, a web of time. It respects time's nuances, its subtle flavors and its many varied relationships.

We moderns have moved far away from the organic time created on the fourth day. We tend to approach time as something that is ours to "use." We imagine we are the center of time, that time revolves around us. Mark Twain captured this sense in his essay, "Was the World Made for Man?":

> Man has been here 32,000 years. That it took a hundred million years to prepare the world for him is proof that that is what it was done for. I suppose it is, I dunno. If the Eiffel Tower were now representing the world's age, the skin of paint on the pinnacle knob at its summit would represent man's share of that age and anybody would perceive that that skin was what the tower was built for. I reckon they would, I dunno.[3]

In our world, time is money and we aspire to control it; we exploit it; we multitask. Speed and efficiency are our primary values. We no longer measure time by the motion of the earth in space, but by the atomic oscillations of a metal called cesium. We're more eager to divide time into smaller and smaller units of nanoseconds and picoseconds than we are to expand our experience of our days and years. The irony is that while we strive for greater efficiency, we feel more stress and have less leisure than any other society in history.

Rabbi Saul Berman recounts that in the early 1970s, with the advent of computer technology and the ability to complete one's work in a fraction of the time, Americans eagerly anticipated a life of leisure, and America's religious leaders debated the consequences of so much freedom. But ultimately the time that technology created only produced higher expectations to work faster and accomplish more. The more time we had, the more money we could make, the more happiness we thought we could acquire.

But happiness has little to do with money and spare time. We speed through time to make money in order to escape a fundamental aloneness at the core of our being, a separation from our souls. We hide from our aloneness by surrounding ourselves with more things, imagining that the more we have, the more we are. We think we can buy a life.

The ideas of "time as money" and "money as the key to happiness" are absent from Hebrew time-consciousness. The word for time in Hebrew is *zeman*, which also means "invitation;" it implies a readiness, an eagerness to respond to whatever time brings. Happiness is related to our enjoyment of the invisible gifts of the moment, not the personality's transitory craving to attain things. Happiness comes with our feelings of gratitude for everything we have been given. The imperative of Jewish consciousness is to choose life, to choose to live the moments of our lives as fully as we can.

When I reflect on my experience of time, I realize that in the periods when I defined my life by my career, I was in a constant state of hurry, flying from one thing to the next, preoccupied by the demands of my job. I rarely had time to chat with my friends and neighbors, to run errands, take care of my home, volunteer in my community. There was a sense of excitement and accomplishment, but also a sense that I was skimming the surface and missing out on the depth of life.

My attitude was nurtured by a family creed that believed the end was more important than the means: as a child I would rush through the tasks and homework of the week to make time to do more important things on the weekend—like ski and play tennis. If I sat still for a moment, I thought I was "killing time."

Today I live with an entirely different time orientation. Now it's important to me to enjoy life's ordinary tasks. I don't want to hurry through the details of my routine activities as if they are interruptions—they compose the fabric of my life. Now, I engage in relationships with the people who fix my car and my house and my body, who sell me my food and my appliances. I want my visits to the mechanic and the dentist and the grocery store to be satisfying. I want to feel the moments spread out before me. I rarely go far away on weekends any more; it's too much work. It's not worth the hours spent in preparation and the hours reorganizing when I return, just to get away—I ask myself, "get away" from what?—for a couple of days. I prefer to stay home and sink deeper into my own life right here right now.

"There is a time for everything under heaven" says the poet Kohelet. I am trying to remember this. I am on the lookout for *otot*, miracles and synchronicities, that remind me of God's presence in my life. I try to ground myself in the *moadim*, seasons, by responding to the different needs of my garden in spring, summer, and fall, wearing colors and fabrics that reflect nature's hues and textures, and celebrating the festivals that mark each season. I think of each *yom*, day, as part of the ocean of time, and a connection to eternity. I reflect on my life through the *shanim*, years, knowing I have constant opportunities to change my life so that it is a better reflection of my deepest desires.

✦

And they will be for **lights** in the expanse of the heaven
to shine upon the earth. And it was so (1.15)

*Ve-hayu li-**meorot** bi-rekia ha-shamayim
lehair al-ha-aretz. Va-yehi-khain.*

THE POWER OF THE SUN

Not only do the heavenly lights provide a time orientation for all
life on earth, they also give light to the earth. Light is the energy
that all creatures live on. Through the process of photosynthesis,
plants "eat" the sun. They capture the sun's light energy and transform it into chemical energy, making food for themselves and for
everyone else. We depend on plants and on the animals that eat
them and on the fuels that we derive from them for every aspect of
our lives.

These days we have distanced ourselves from the sun. We use
fossil fuels, not sunlight, to warm our homes and power our gadgets. We imagine that we're dependent on these resources and that
the quality of our lives would suffer without them. From an ecological and an economic perspective it makes little sense to exploit
fossil fuels and pollute our environment when the sun can provide
all the energy we need in the form of direct light energy.[4] Solar energy is free; there's no nasty pollution and it's sustainable. It is the
perfect energy source.

The technology to utilize solar energy exists in the form of
solar thermal collectors, wind turbines, and photovoltaic cells (roof
panels to capture sunlight). But we continue to use fossil fuels,
which are costly, wasteful, limited in supply, and toxic to our health
and environment. Ultimately politics and calcified ways of thinking
get in the way of our conversion to solar power.

❧

And God made the **two great lights**
the **greater light to rule the day;** and the **smaller light
to rule the night,** and the stars (1.16)

*Va-ya'as Elohim et **shenai ha-meorot ha-gedolim**
et-**ha-maor ha-gadol lememshelet ha-yom** ve-et-**ha-maor ha-katan**
lememshelet ha-laylah ve-et ha-kokhavim.*

❧

THE CYCLES OF THE SUN AND THE MOON

We are ruled by the sun and the moon, but we hardly notice. We are calibrated by the rhythms of nature. The cycles of time provide the structure, the anatomy, the heartbeat for all life on earth.

The earth's revolution around the sun gives us the year and its seasons. Depending on the position of the earth relative to the sun, temperatures change and days lengthen or shorten. Day length triggers a host of changes in the earth's creatures. As the days get shorter, migratory birds fatten up and shift their sleep/wake cycle (they sleep by day and fly by night, taking advantage of the stars of the night sky), bear and squirrels hibernate, weasels change color, and many people turn inward (while our culture views the depression that sometimes accompany winter as an illness and labels it seasonal affective disorder, SAD, other cultures would recognize such depression as the appropriate state of being for winter). As days lengthen, crocuses and daffodils bloom, bears come out of their lairs, and people smile more.

The earth's revolution around its own axis gives us the day and we're also tied to this cycle. Most creatures follow a twenty-four-hour cycle of daytime activity and nighttime rest. Eighteenth-century naturalists were intrigued by these rhythms. Observing the sleep and wake cycles of flowers, botanist Carolus Lineus suggested that you could actually tell time by paying attention to a garden, and he conceived of a "flower clock."

At 6 A.M. spotted cat's ear opens; 7 A.M. African marigold opens; 8 A.M. mouse ear hawkweed opens; 9 A.M. prickly snowthistle closes; 10 A.M. common nipplewort closes; 11 A.M. star of Bethlehem opens; 12 noon passion flower opens . . .[5]

Our energy levels also cycle according to the daily rhythms. We're usually more aware of this when we're ill—sometimes we notice that we feel worse in the evening or morning or at a particular hour during the day.

The moon's rotation round the earth gives us the month and inscribes in us another cycle. The idea of moon as a measure of time is still embedded in our speech. In most European languages, the word month comes from *me* or *men*, meaning measure. (In Hebrew, "moon," and "month" are related to the word *yerach*, travel; the month is determined by the moon's regular trip around the earth. In ancient times, Jews based their calendar on the moon).

When the moon travels round the earth, it exerts a rhythmic pull, tugging at the oceans, causing a cycle in the tides. The swarming, spawning, and mating of many sea creatures are related to these fluctuations.

In fact, the moon pulls at all liquid on earth, and because we humans are mostly made of water, we can sense this pull. Women's menstrual cycle is the most obvious expression of the hold the moon has on us. Folk wisdom describes women's bodies waxing and waning with the cycle of the moon, filling up as the moon fills and spilling out as the moon dims. The relationship is not just physiological. There is a sense of turning inward with the moon's darkening—ultimately to the menstrual hut for reflection and inner examination—and turning outwards with the moon's brightening, ready to mate.[6] I am told that if we aren't already tuned in to the moon's cycle, we can train our bodies to track the moon by sleeping with a lit lamp in our rooms during the days of the full moon.

Male or female, we are governed by the moon. We may grow livelier as the moon brightens and quieter as the moon dims.

Psychiatric hospitals and police departments report that wild, spirited behavior, auto accidents, and crimes increase with the full moon. The word lunacy itself originally referred to bizarre behaviors brought on by the full moon.

✦

Jewish life has always been governed by the moon. The ancients honored the two nodes of life, emptiness and fullness: the new moon and the full moon. They proclaimed the new moon with bonfires, establishing it as a holy day, a day free from work for women, and they set most festivals on the full moon.

In ancient times, astronomy was part of a rabbi's vocation and moon-watching was a regular part of peoples' lives. The Talmud depicts Rabbi Gamliel's study, replete with drawings of the phases of the moon displayed so that moon-watchers could accurately describe their sightings. It was a mitzvah to bear witness to the new moon, and people would journey long distances to Jerusalem to report their findings. Accounting for the new moon was so important that travelers, eager to testify, were allowed to travel on Shabbat (it is customarily forbidden to ride or exchange money on the Sabbath) and were rewarded with a great feast when they arrived in the holy city.

Today, artificial lights, indoor living, and irregular work hours obscure our possibilities for a connection with the moon and the cycles of nature. The invention of the clock in the thirteenth century and, with it, the human-made hour—the first nonnaturally derived unit of time—initiated the trend away from cyclical time and toward linear time. In the nineteenth century the introduction of electric lights reinforced this attitude and altered the daily rhythm of time forever. And this is a tragedy. We have abstracted time from its "natural" context, from its smells and tastes and lights and seasons, and have grown more and more separate from nature.

We moderns live by time's arrow, largely unconscious of time's cycle. A strict linear time orientation can lead to the illusion that we humans control time and that "progress" is the ultimate virtue. The earth suffers from such anti-ecological values and so do we. Living lives based on constant forward movement leads to stress and a whole host of chronic illnesses like Epstein Barr and chronic fatigue syndrome. One hundred years ago, doctors would send their patients to spas where they would eat, sleep, and wake at prescribed hours, in part to help them recalibrate their internal rhythms, which fall out of synch when the body's cyclical needs for rest and sleep are ignored.

Fortunately, Jewish tradition maintains much of the legacy of cyclical time today. We still celebrate most festivals in tune with the full moon. Many Jewish women pay homage to the new moon by gathering together at Rosh Hodesh, the first day of each Jewish month. Some of us still honor the daily cycle according to tradition by reciting our prayers at dawn and dusk.

The guideposts exist in our traditions to help us lead lives that are healthy, rich, and ecologically sound—it's up to us to integrate the wisdom and practices into our lives and give them our own meaning.

And God **gave** them to the expanse of the heaven
to light up the earth (1.17)[7]

*Va-**yitain** otam Elohim bi-rekiya ha-shamayim
lehair al-ha-aretz.*

THE GIFT OF TIME, THE PRACTICE OF PRAYER

The word *yitain* is a form of the word "to give" in Hebrew. It has the same root as the word, *natan*, gift. The luminaries, and the dimensions of time they create, are a gift from God.

We rarely approach time as a gift. Unlike many of the gifts of creation that we can see and touch, time is imperceptible. Because it is vast and invisible, we imagine it stretches on forever ahead of us and behind us, and too often we take it for granted.

The idea of time as a gift is powerful both spiritually and eco-logically. If we could fill ourselves with the invisible moments of time, rather than the material artifacts of space, we might discover a new fulfillment as we deepen our care for nature.

Time (*zeman*) is an invitation (*zeman*) to encounter all the mys-teries a moment brings. We can relish time, awake and aware, choosing life in every moment, or we can let time pass by, reacting unconsciously to our circumstances.

Responding to time doesn't mean using time to accomplish or accumulate; it doesn't mean doing more in less time. It means simply being in time. It means experiencing time fully—being aware of whatever feelings and thoughts—good or bad—time offers us, and integrating them all. It means living with the presence of the present.

We are invited to discover, uncover, and explore the gifts of time and all of nature, to turn them over and around, to treasure them. We are invited to wonder at all we have been given.

Time becomes a gift only when it has a receiver. When a gift is offered and it is not received, it becomes an object with no particu-lar meaning. It loses its power as a gift. We cannot receive if our hearts are hard. The gift may be delivered, but the door is closed.

Many of us are not receptive to gifts freely given. We think that the only rewards come from our own willfulness. Every day we gird ourselves for battle to advance and progress; we tense our shoulders, tighten our jaws, furrow our brows, and harden our hearts. We become used to a constant state of defensiveness, never availing ourselves to the gifts all around.

Prayer is a practice of opening the door, opening the heart to welcome the gifts. In Hebrew, to pray, *lehitpalel*, is a reflexive verb, something we do to ourselves, like wash or dress. It requires prac-tice, like playing an instrument or learning a language. When our hearts soften, our bodies open and we can receive the gifts.

The rabbis composed blessings—for rain (which as desert dwellers they understood as "good news"), the ocean, mountains, valleys, shooting stars, thunder, and lightning—to train us to open our hearts to the Creator's gifts. They gave us a simple practice to help us to meet the world afresh with beginner's eyes. Upon seeing mountains, valleys, oceans, rivers, and wilderness, for example, we say, "Praise to You who makes the works of creation."[8]

While prayer is the practice of receiving, it is also the practice of giving. If the fundamental human flaw is our insistence that the world is ours to take, then the fundamental repair requires our giving back to the world. The rabbis believed that one way to give back is to pause throughout the day to express gratitude. They suggested making one hundred blessings a day to train us to remember the myriad of gifts and to return the gift by pouring back our love. We're to do this even when we're not in the mood for gratitude, even when the world looks bleak.

My favorite Jewish teaching is probably the most obvious one: *Yehudim*, the Hebrew word for Jews, means to give thanks; *yehuda* is related to *todah*, "thank you." My friend Gershon Winkler says being a Jew means first and foremost being a "thanks-giver." This is our obligation. It's time for Jews to adopt this as a slogan, the watchword of our faith. An attitude of gratitude provides the foundation for our caring for the world.

Prayer or any form of quiet contemplation can center a stewardship practice. It can help us overcome our narcissism and our indifference to creation; it can sensitize us to the world. It can help us regard all of life as a gift and teach us to care for it.

Lately I've been using the first few words from Psalm 23— "The Lord is my shepherd, I shall not want"—as a mantra to focus my mind and keep my heart open to the creation's gifts. I love the imagery of God as a shepherd. Shepherding was considered the lowliest of tasks of ancient Israel, the most earthbound, the closest to the ground. If God is my shepherd, then I am a sheep. As I lay myself down, outstretched on the bosom of the earth, I smell the sweetness of the dew and feel the coolness of the earth. The emerald green meadows, flecked with wild flowers, roll out before me. And I realize, what more could I want? I am hopelessly provided for.

Traditional prayers in all religions include bowing postures and prostrations. As we lower our heads beneath our hearts, we are brought down to our humble roots and reminded that we are not masters of the universe. I never knew that this idea was alive in Judaism until I conducted a survey of the psalms that are chanted for the Friday night service, kabbalat Shabbat, literally the service for "receiving" the Sabbath, the ultimate gift of time. The practice of bowing down, of falling on your face in devotion, in recognition of the mystery of life, is noted in six of the seven psalms that we chant as we welcome Shabbat. We don't perform the motions any more, nor do we bang the cymbals or play the trumpet or the shofar to herald the Sabbath Queen, but I imagine if we did we would have a whole new experience of humility and grace.

It's not just to purify ourselves, not just to see the world anew, that we pray. Nature needs us to give back. The cycle of giving and receiving must be complete. The Talmud said that it is forbidden to enjoy anything without blessing it first. If you eat a fruit and neglect to make a *bracha*, blessing, to express your gratitude, you are like a robber. The plant needs your energy to bring forth a new generation of fruit, and by not blessing, you rob it of its energy. You have taken from the plant and not given back.[9] The expression of gratitude (or lack of it) has material consequences in the world. So religions provide us with prayers to say every time we eat or partake of the gifts of creation, to remind us where our food comes from and to teach us to complete the eternal cycle of giving and receiving.

Prayer and blessings are religion's ways of bounding off palatable slices of time, of ritualizing particular moments, to capture them and lift them up from the ocean of time. When we see the blessedness of certain moments, we become more open to the possibility of blessedness in all moments. Most traditions set particular hours of the day for prayer. The Benedictines observe fixed times for waking, working, praying, eating, and resting; every hour has its purpose.[10]

Dawn and dusk are common times for prayer in all traditions. Many people experience a sublime sense of life's mystery and a deep peace at sunrise or sunset when earth is changing from light to dark or dark to light. We see more clearly when the light is not overhead but when we are losing it or gaining it, when it is balanced with a touch of darkness. These transition times provide a window to holiness and an opportunity for seeing more deeply.

I have always been a morning person; I'm up with the birds to watch the daybreak. The beauty of these hours finds their way into my heart, and I am moved, basking in gratitude for the life I have been given. In my courting stages with Judaism, I was gratified that my tradition marked these times with prayers that expressed what I could not find words for.

> Source of Blessing, Eternal God, Master of the Universe;
> You form light and create darkness, make peace and create
>   everything.
> How great are Your works, O God,
> in wisdom You have made them all;
> the earth is full of Your possessions.
> You give light out of mercy to the earth
> and in Your goodness You renew creation every day . . . [11]

I like to use the traditional hours that the rabbis designated as prayer times to tune into my soul and the soul of the world. This way I can connect with the cosmic world and my ancestors at the same time, joining my prayers with theirs and with all of the natural world.

Today people go to great lengths and spend small fortunes pursuing all kinds of therapies and self-help technologies to find a connection to the world and to identify their life purpose. We're so used to our purchasing power that we think we can go to market to acquire an identity.

But our identities are wrapped up in what we value, our relations, and how we spend our time. The practice of prayer in all traditions has helped to sustain people and taught them to live meaningful lives for thousands of years. When we take time for quiet prayer and reflection every day, we can get in touch with our deepest values, our true identity, and honor our bond with nature.

૭ુ

And to rule over the day and over the night
and to divide between the light and the darkness.
And God saw that it was **good.** (1.18)

Ve-limshol ba-yom u-va-laylah
u-lehavdil bain ha-or u-vain ha-choshekh.
*Ve-yar Elohim ki-***tov.**

૭ુ

GOOD AND HOLY DAYS

The obvious response to the "goodness" of the fourth day is to celebrate, especially since the festivals, the *moadim*, are also created on this day (see 1.14). In Hebrew *moadim* is the word for both season and festival; the festivals are the hidden gifts of the heavenly lights.

Many years ago I asked my friend Jeffrey Dekro, a pretty serious guy, what was compelling to him about Judaism, and he answered very simply, "it's fun." I couldn't believe my ears. Judaism, fun? Meaningful, yes; transformative, maybe; but fun? I realized that he was talking about the holidays, but I had never had any fun on a Jewish holiday before; I had known them as solemn, mournful, or boring occasions. Still, I thought he might be on to something and I began to explore for myself.

Over time, I understood that the holidays were not, as I had once thought, isolated moments that fell randomly throughout the year, commemorating historical events to which I felt no connection. The festivals marked the seasons—the joy of rain at its proper time, the ingathering of an abundant harvest and the birthing of the lambs—long before they were associated with historical significance. The holy days were bound to each other and to the world in a grand seasonal tapestry. And while we are not connected to nature in the way our ancestors were, and few of us depend on the agricultural cycle for our livelihood, the light of the holy days, the light shed by the sun and the moon on these special occasions, can capture the moods of the different seasons and connect us to nature and our souls.

While I was exploring the possibilities of the holy days of my own tradition, artist Chris Wells was teaching me about how pageantry and parades—the holy day festivities in other traditions—can capture the imagination of an entire community and move them towards an ecological vision and practice. Having participated in the festivals of many native cultures in South America, Chris decided that what the earth needed was its own holy day and he created All Species Day. His goal was to raise the community's consciousness about the wonder and diversity of life and to engage them in its protection. Every year the folks at the All Species Project would work with the schools and community groups to generate interest in the species and habitats of the world, and every spring the residents of Santa Fe, old and young alike, would don their homemade, environmentally friendly creature costumes and gather together on foot, in carriages, on stilts, in wheelbarrows, on roller blades, on bicycle, or on horseback to proudly participate in the All Species Parade.

Chris taught me about the power of holy day festivals to pull a community together and transmit a serious ecological message within a celebratory context. Joyful and meaningful holiday celebrations can crack open our hearts and minds and begin to change our attitudes and behaviors so that we make better choices for ourselves and the earth. Contrast this with the kind of religious moral education that too often yields a negative reaction.

When I founded the Jewish environmental organization Shomrei Adamah, Keepers of the Earth, I was convinced that the Jewish holy days offered a treasure chest of wisdom and practices that could be used in the service of Judaism's spiritual heritage and in service of the earth, and I began to explore the possibilities.

Tu B'Sh'vat, the Jewish new year of the trees, does not imme-diately come to mind when you think of the Jewish holy days. It was neglected for most of the twentieth century, relegated to pedi-atric status as a tree-planting day for children. But it is, in fact, the perfect environmental holy day, a time to celebrate nature and our soulful connection to it.

Established in rabbinic times as a day to pay taxes on the fruit trees, Tu B'Sh'vat was invigorated by the kabbalists, the mystics of Safed, in the 1600s. They created a seder, a ritual following a par-ticular order, to celebrate the day. You can imagine a Tu B'Sh'vat seder as a four-course ritual meal organized around the kabbalistic four worlds of *atzilut* (spirit), *briyah* (thought), *yetzirah* (emotion), and *assiyah* (doing)—each course consisting of biblical and mysti-cal readings about nature, garnished with fruits, wines, and bless-ings. The more fruit you eat and the more wine you drink, the more blessings you're required to say, the more the earth is healed.

I was eager to develop a Tu B'Sh'vat ritual that could evoke the kind of mystical experience of soul and nature envisioned by the kabbalists, and at the same time lift Tu B'Sh'vat out of relative ob-scurity and provide it the visibility it deserves.

My desire was to create, in ecophilosopher David Abram's words, a "spell of the sensuous." Because a "sense of place" is such a subtle but vital aspect of ecological (and I might add religious) ed-ucation, I chose to set my first seder in one of Philadelphia's boat-houses on the banks of the Schuylkill River. In this seder, the kab-balistic four worlds translate naturally into the elements of earth, water, air, and fire and they set the stage for the ritual drama. Artists in the community decorated the space and created a virtual Garden of Eden, a garden of earthly and heavenly delights. The two hun-dred guests at the seder took on the characters of creatures from the worlds of earth, water, air, or fire and dressed accordingly. People entered the space and took their places in silence. World by world, we read from the seder, ate fruit, and drank wine, listened to musi-cal offerings composed by local musicians, sang, and laughed. And world by world, we observed stillness, contemplated our place in nature, and made blessings. Integrating pageantry, art, and theater along with religious insights and ecological understandings, we created a beautiful and evocative new ritual for Tu B'Sh'vat.

According to the kabbalists, the point of the seder is to repair the world. Repair of the world begins with repair of our minds. On Tu B'Sh'vat we are asked to overcome the fundamental flaw of our consciousness (that began when Adam ate the apple): our belief that we are the masters of creation and that the earth belongs to us. "The earth belongs to God," sang the psalmist. We are all part of one interwoven system and we all belong to God. The seder provides the context for us to recognize our utter dependence on the Creator for all the fruits of creation. Through our blessings and our humility we give back in gratitude to the Maker of all, and so participate in the process of repair.

Just as Tu B'Sh'vat offers a way for us to tune into the soul of the world and our own souls and practice *tikkun*, or repair, so do many holy days in all traditions. In Jewish tradition, the holy days—particularly the "high holidays" (Rosh Hashanah, Yom Kippur) and the agricultural holidays (Succot, Passover, and Shavuot)—can act as a compass to orient us to who we are and where we're going in our personal and spiritual lives at periodic intervals throughout the year. Festivals are invitations to capture the seasonal moments and celebrate them.

The Jewish year, Rosh Hashanah, begins in the fall as the days are growing shorter. Flowers have peaked and gone to seed, and nature is turning inwards, preparing for winter. All the world is in a state of change. Rabbi David Zeller calls Rosh Hashanah (literally head/*rosh* of the year/*shana*) "Change Head" day, because *shana* also means "to change." The autumn welcomes the change, blows off our dead leaves, and invites us go inside to change our minds (abandon the hold societal norms have on us) and return to our true being in preparation for the next round of life. The renewal in nature invites the renewal of our souls.

Sukkot, following on the heels of the New Year, is the harvest fest and the beginning of the rainy season: time to gather in the fruits and vegetables of the year's labors. This is Judaism's original enironmental holiday and Thanksgiving. Many Jews construct flimsy little huts called sukkot to commemorate the shacks the ancient Israelites built to store their harvest (some say sukkot commemorate the journey in wilderness).

With its festive decorations—like twinkly lights and miniature pumpkins—and its unassuming posture, the sukkah has always found its way into my heart. It's a mitzvah to make the sukkah beautiful, and in Mt. Airy, we enjoy a friendly sukkah decorating competition. My friend Anna fancies herself a Jewish Martha Stewart and she's always concocting new Sukkot recipes using green beans, squash, potatoes, and fresh herbs from her garden, and decorating her sukkah with makeshift window dressings of cheery fabrics she finds hidden away in a closet. One year I grew a garden full of gourds just to have exotic decorations for my sukkah. Now I cultivate many late blooming flowers: cleome, Mexican sunflower, zinnias, goldenrod, boltonia, and asters. I collect seed pods—the best are blackberry lilies—grasses, and spent yarrow, and make lavish bouquets to hang upside down from the rafters.

In this neighborhood on the Saturday afternoon of Sukkot (Sukkot lasts eight days), you'll see hundreds of people enjoying the annual sukkah walk, strolling, biking, and pushing carriages up and down the streets, admiring the simple beauty of each sukkah, delighting in the bounty (we all cook up a storm; my standard is sweet potato soup), and the pleasure of the company. On Sukkot, you're actually commanded to be joyful. I love this idea. It's as if we've forgotten how to be happy and must be taught. The Bible says that true joy comes by inviting all of your friends, including your long-departed ancestors, and a few strangers to squeeze into your open-air hut for a big picnic or a sleepover, no matter rain or shine.

At the end of Sukkot comes Simchat Torah, and with it one of the most beautiful prayers in all of Jewish liturgy—the prayer for rain. This prayer eloquently expresses our utter dependence on God for rain and water and food and life. And this is cause for celebration. In my community everyone—old and young alike—join in the wild singing and dancing (a little schnapps helps those who are stiffer). On Simchat Torah, more than at any other time in the calendar, I have a fleeting glimpse of God's presence in the world. I get a little giddy seeing that my community's renewal is inextricably tied to the renewal of the land, food, and rains. We are indeed one.

Passover heralds the end of the winter rains, the beginning of spring, time to embrace our freedom and pay attention to the ripening grains. My most memorable Passover was a backpacking trip in the Grand Canyon with a group of science teachers about twenty-five years ago. While we were all enjoying our hike through geologic time, in my imagination, I was also reenacting the Exodus. I wanted to live the experience of liberation on a trek through the wilderness.

My new friends were eager to celebrate Passover too so I instructed them in the symbols of Passover and sent them on a scavenger hunt to discover what artifacts they might find for the seder plate. They returned laden with various skeletal remains licked clean by wolves to serve as shankbone(s), a variety of greens for karpas, sage for bitter herbs, and Indian paintbrush and other wildflowers for a festive centerpiece. I had brought a few pieces of matzah and some apples and nuts for haroset. As the sun set we gathered together for a homemade vegetable feast cooked over a little camp stove. We found a beautiful spot where the red canyon wall formed an overhang to protect us from any possible rain, and there, cradled in the most awesome river canyon with the full moon rising overhead, we sat and talked the night away, asking and answering questions, eating, and telling stories of our own liberation.

Passover is not just a holy day in and of itself; it is the beginning of the observance of the season of spring. It marks the start of the *omer*, the forty-nine-day period between Passover and Shavuot when the Israelites watched and waited for their spring grains to sprout and grow. The ancients were understandably apprehensive about their crops at this time and they marked each day. Too much rain in spring could ruin the tender shoots of wheat and barley; no grain meant there would be no bread in the coming year.

In medieval times, the mystics who lived in cities did not till the soil, yet they still took the *omer* seriously, counting the days between Passover and Shavuot. They were on the lookout for the hidden energies, the subtle nuances of each day. They believed that the *omer* period was the time for personal transformation. Just as the vigorous trek through the empty wilderness had the effect of cleansing the Israelites so that they could receive the Torah at Mount Sinai with a pure heart, the kabbalists felt we all can purify ourselves by invoking the energies of each day of the *omer* in preparation for the revelation on Shavuot. They developed a mystical calendar by which we could tap into the subtle qualities of the days, and so transform ourselves.

Shavuot marks the end of the *omer* and with it the ripening of the wheat and God's revelation of the Torah to the people. It is time to bake two loaves of wheat bread to offer up in gratitude for the rain in its proper season, two loaves to give back to complete the cycle of life, the cycle of giving and receiving.

The last of the holidays of the Jewish year is Tisha B'Av. Although a minor holiday, it holds ecological significance for me. It falls in midsummer, invariably during a Philadelphia heat wave— this year we're in the midst of the worst drought we've had since the '60s. Pennsylvania's primary income is from agriculture, and all of our crops are withering. My garden is parched and so am I. People are even selling their livestock. These are the dog days of summer. I don't have to look at the calendar to know Tisha B'Av is coming. Tisha B'Av remembers the destruction of both of the ancient Temples (in 546 and 70 B.C.E.), the breakdown of Judaism's center, the drying up of the wellspring of life. It is a time of profound grief and loss, of haunting mournful laments. I am always more acutely aware of our environmental vulnerability this time of year. But I pray that in the cycle of life we will overcome our harmful, self-indulgent ways, and we and the land will have the opportunity to begin again. Rosh Hashanah is just around the bend and with it the promise of life-giving rains and a new year.

✦

Sadly, most Jewish communities—out of convenience and habit—observe the holidays indoors, cut off from the moods, smells, and flavors of the particular time of year. In such a setting, the observance of the holidays invariably becomes more of a mental exercise—a remembrance of time past, rather than a celebration of time present. When the holidays are cut off from their natural context, people sense that something is wrong—they feel disconnected. Outside of their natural context, the prayers lose their meaning and flavor—they are like an empty shell. It is no wonder that Jewish leaders are perplexed as to why modern synagogue life, by and large, isn't able to capture the imagination of the masses of Jews.

The festival days were designed to orient us to the nuances of time and the cycles of nature. When we celebrate the holidays in their seasonal glory, they become saturated with meaning and irresistible to child and adult alike.

❧

And there was evening and there was morning, a fourth day. (1.19)

Va-yehi-erev va-yehi-voker yom revi'i.

❧

EVERY DAY A NEW DAY

We often take our days for granted, thinking this day will be the same as the last, business as usual, another day in the convention of our lives. But our days are our own to live out as we will—time is the only "thing" that truly belongs to us. Every day we can choose how we will spend our hours; we can alter our whole existence in one day.

The rabbis said that you can even change your life on the day that you die. Every day is a whole new story, an entire lifetime.

Every day we are given the opportunity to start fresh again. Each night, we go to sleep and the soul departs, journeying to distant places, learning, changing, developing. Each morning we wake up and the soul is restored. It is a new day and anything is possible. Great transformations take place in the dark; we can awake a new person.

Each day is a universe unto itself. Every day an opportunity to transform ourselves. It is never too late to be what we could have been.

Time, and how we relate to it, is as important as space in the ecological equation. Each day we can love our neighbor, leave a stale job, follow our dreams, simplify our lives, fix up a house in the city, plant a garden, teach a child to read, engage in community, dance, paint, write, join the school board, call a congressperson, give *tzedakah* / charity. There are hundreds of ways to honor our days and express our gratitude for the multitude of gifts we are constantly given.

✽

WATER AND WIND CREATURES

THE FIFTH DAY

And God said, "Let the water swarm
with living swarming soul(s), and let flyer(s) fly
above the earth in the expanse of the sky."

And God created the great sea monsters,
and every living soul that creeps that the waters
swarmed forth after their kind,
and every winged flyer after its kind.
And God saw that it was good.

And God blessed them, saying,
"Be fruitful and multiply and replenish
the waters in the seas and let the flyer
multiply in the earth."

And there was evening and
there was morning, a fifth day.

꙳

And God said, "Let the waters **swarm** with living **swarming soul(s),**[1] and let **flyer(s) fly** above the earth in the expanse of the sky." (1.20)

Va-yomer Elohim yishretzu ha-mayim sheretz nefesh chayah ve-of yeofaif al-ha-aretz al-penai rekia ha-shamayim.

꙳

CREATURES IN MOTION

After God establishes the elemental infrastructure—light, air, water, earth, plants, and time—the animals appear. "If you build it, they will come." The order of creation, once again, corresponds to the sequence of evolution.

Animals are distinguished from all that has come before them by their ability to move independently. Plants, after all, never venture forth from the ground in which they are rooted, except as seeds. They move in response to the sun or, in the case of carnivorous plants, in response to their prey. But if you're not a plant and can't manufacture your own food, moving about to find food is key to staying alive.

Indeed the creatures on the fifth day are described in terms of movement: there are swarming swarmers and flying flyers. The Hebrew roots that express motion are repeated—*sheretz* yi*shretzu* and *of* ye*ofaif*—emphasizing the centrality of movement to animal life.

Animal movement is a function of both form and habitat. Fish are designed for water and birds for air. Habitat is so important in the Genesis story, that creatures are even identified by their particular "place." The story describes flying flyers of the *sky* and swarming souls of the *waters*, not just birds and fish. The human *earthling*— *adam* in Hebrew—is also named for its place—*adamah*, or earth.

The significance of place cannot be underestimated. The various places of creation actually collaborate with God to create the forms that will move in and through them. Water "swarms forth" swimming (swarming) creatures, and earth "brings forth" plants and walking creatures. Water and air flow in spirals, waves, and circles, and the watery and airy creatures embody these flowing forms. Birds, fish, and snakes create undulating and spiraling patterns as they move through the fluids they inhabit.

Each habitat presents challenges and opportunities. Those forms that fit the environment (flyers for air, swimmers for sea) will move gracefully in it and will find food, reproduce, and thrive. Those that do not will eventually disappear. Such is the Genesis version of natural selection. According to the rabbis:

> You have creatures that grow in the sea and creatures that grow on dry land. If those of the sea were to come up on dry land they would die immediately. If those of the dry land were to go down into the sea they would die. . . . The place of life for one is the cause of death for the other.[2]

Fish, designed for living in water, a medium eight hundred times denser than air, have streamlined bodies and minimized appendages so they can cut through their fluid surroundings with ease. They swim by undulating their bodies, in harmony with the rhythm of the water itself.[3] Flyers, designed for air, have winged forelimbs and small hollow bones enabling them to get off the ground and stay aloft. Amphibians, like frogs, who must navigate two entirely different environments, spend the first part of their lives streamlined to accommodate a watery habitat, and the latter part with legs for hopping about the earth.

The multitude of habitats provides the impetus for the remarkable adaptations in animal form and locomotion. This is most apparent in land animals. Cheetahs, who can travel at speeds of eighty miles per hour to outrun their prey, have long sinewy legs, made longer as they dislocate and relocate their backs with each stride. Burrowers, like gophers, have short stubby appendages, excellent for digging underground. Large lumbering creatures, like elephants, can afford to be heavy; their very size repels predators.

I used to think animal form and movement was all about utility: each creature's adaptations to its particular niche enabled the animal an ability to find food or protect itself. But animal movement is also

a matter of communication, an outward expression of an inward
state. Motion is a reflection of e-motion. The muscles that enable
creatures to move also express what is in their hearts / minds.

Motion and emotion are intimately linked with the soul's desire. In this verse, the swimming creatures are referred to as *nefesh*,
which can be translated as soul, desire, or creature. The creatures
communicate their soul's desire through movement. They move towards what they like and away from what they dislike; they flare
their nostrils when angry; puff themselves up if threatened; go limp
to convey surrender; and perform elaborate dance rituals to court a
mate. Similarly, human animals communicate through muscles. Our
facial muscles and even the muscles of our bodies express a whole
range of feelings, whether we are aware of it or not.

Animals in motion are also a matter of beauty. The rabbis said
that *yishretzu ha mayim sheretz,* generally translated as, "Let the waters swarm with swarmers" can also mean "Let the water draw pic-
tures."⁴ Indeed, fish in motion, and by extension the birds and all the
animals, are nature's works of art.

And God created the great sea monsters,
and every living soul that creeps that the waters swarmed forth
after their kind, and every winged flyer after its kind.
And God saw that it was good. (1.21)

*Va-***yivra** *Elohim et-***ha-tanninim ha-gedolim**
ve-et-kol-nefesh ha-chayah ha-romeset asher sharetzu ha-mayim
le-minaihem ve-et kol-of kanaf le-minaihu.
Va-yar Elohim ki-tov.

GOD AT PLAY

In such a carefully planned and highly ordered creation story characterized by parallels of matching kinds—night and day, heaven

above and waters below, the grasses and fruit trees, sun and moon, an ocean of swarming creatures and a sky of flying creatures—the abrupt appearance of the *tanninim*, variously translated as sea monsters, dinosaurs, and whales, is particularly striking.

While the very existence of the sea monsters is startling, the way in which they are formed is also surprising. God *bara*'ed/created the sea monsters. The word *bara* (root form of *yivra*) or create has actually only been used once so far in the creation story. In the first verse of the Bible God *bara*'ed/created heaven and earth. "*Bara*" refers to creation out of nothing. Only God can *bara*; people can not.

In the whole of creation, the sea monster and later humankind are directly *bara*'ed by God. God formed much of the rest of creation simply by dividing up the original matter or collaborating on the job with the habitats.

Why is the sea monster so special?[5] Some say the sea creatures are singled out, in part, for their enormous size; they are of mythic proportion, the only animals in the creation story described as "great/*gedolim*."

Others say that the sea monster was especially created as a playmate for God. In Psalm 104, the sea monster, Leviathan, is the one with whom God frolics in the sea. While God is clearly concerned with planning and ordering the universe, God also needs to play. After all, too much order can lead to the ordinary. Creation is also about pleasure and mystery and surprise.

We tend to dismiss the value of play, assuming it's really just for kids. Caught up in our work (oh-so-important) and our responsibilities, many of us grow unnecessarily uptight and joyless.

The sea monster reminds us that our responsibility, our ability to respond, to creation includes playing with her. Playing in creation is an antidote for overactive minds that keep us bound to the conventions of the world. At play in nature, we can retrieve our innocence, our dreams and our joy, our possibilities.

It is no coincidence that play is associated with this day, the day symbolized by Movement. "Play" according to Webster refers to "action, motion, or activity especially when free, rapid, or light."

Play is pleasurable because our movement liberates us. While children and some adults find "sitting still" to be a form of torture, running, swimming, climbing, and dancing are considered the greatest pleasures. Sport is really just an excuse to go outdoors and use our limbs for what they were actually designed: to experience the simple but sublime pleasure of the body in motion.

Play is the primary activity of all creatures that move. Animals spend relatively little time engaged in serious survival activities. Rather they while away their hours running, flying, or hopping about in no particular direction, simply moved by the spirit of enjoyment.

It seems odd to build a case for play and for pleasure, but our culture is so wedded to the idea that happiness comes from weight of owning things, rather than from the pure lightness of being, that real play is entirely undervalued, and its importance must be stressed. Play has no agenda other than a deepened relationship or experience either to nature or another person or oneself. There is nothing to be gained, no money to be made, no one and nothing to be "used." Play offers a way to develop, in Martin Buber's words, a sense of everyone and everything as "thou," or friend, rather than as "it" or thing.

Playing outdoors can help us to develop our own organic relationships with nature so that environment becomes a part of the everyday context of our lives and a regular part of our thoughts, rather than a distant "cause" in a faraway place.

Play also has value beyond the immediate pleasure it brings. The most compelling environmental solutions arise out of play, out of our own stories and experiences in nature, not out of dire threats about the end of the earth or crusades to save a particular creature. When we are at play, when our minds have stopped judging and comparing, creativity flows. At play, scientists and artists create; at play, God created the sea monster.

The stories of play, creativity, and resourcefulness in the face of today's daunting ecological challenge are abundant, and we must retell them in schools, religious institutions, and homes in order to instill hope and possibility in the minds and hearts of our young people. Personal stories of hope can remind us that individuals can make a difference.

The same Creativity that created the sea monsters created us; and our creative potential is infinite. There is always enough creativity to go around; we don't need to compete for it. It is the birthright of every human being. The intuitive and creative solutions that arise out of one individual's vision often have the power to capture the imaginations and invigorate and sustain us in our efforts to live ecological lives. Moreover, creativity, like play, is contagious; one individual's great ideas inspires others. With such a precious and rich inheritance, we should feel confident that our creativity will lead us to discover ways to enjoy healthful and sustainable lives for generations to come.

⤆

And God **blessed** them saying,
"**Be fruitful and multiply** and **replenish** the waters in the seas
and let the flyer **multiply** in the earth." (1. 22)

*Va-***yevarekh** *otam Elohim laimor,*
Peru u-revu u-milu *et-ha-mayim ba-yamim*
ve-ha-of **yirev** *ba-aretz.*

⤆

SUSTAINING CREATION: THE FRUITFULNESS PRINCIPLE

Creativity is a biological necessity as well as an artistic one. While Genesis never mentions other physiological functions, it is preoccupied with fertility, the ultimate form of creativity. Even the name for the sea creatures, *sheretz*, connotes teeming, ceaseless life. God creates and the creatures procreate.

In this verse, God bestows the first blessing to insure that re-creation actually happens. In the blessing lies the promise of abundance, plenty, and fullness.

Yet, one wonders why fish and the birds need "a blessing" to create more of themselves in the first place; isn't sex a most natural and desirable activity? Maybe; maybe not. Evolutionary biologists argue that from a cost-benefit analysis no sex makes more sense. Sex is expensive in terms of time spent looking for a proper partner and energy required for the act of sex itself.

We humans know more than we want to about the effort required for sex. Most of us, from the time of puberty onward, are preoccupied, first with finding a mate, and then with keeping him or her—not to mention the act of mating itself. It's no easier for other species: consider the peacock; it bears the burden of an elaborately designed tail-feather apparatus just for the purpose of seduction.

But biologically speaking, for the sake of the future, sex is a necessity. When two molecules of error-laden DNA come together through sex, they become whole. Sex makes healthy genes. In the long view, sex is the driving force for the unfolding of life. So it is no wonder that God offered a blessing for fertility.

Thousands of years ago the rabbis recognized that even though fish could reproduce on their own, they would need a blessing in order to create enough progeny to fulfill their mandate to fill up or replenish the oceans.[6] The blessing would insure that the fish would be able to reproduce enough of their kinds to survive the hazards of their daily environment: some would be eaten, some would die from disease, and some would drift into threatening surroundings.[7] Mackerel, for example, lay millions of eggs, yet for each million, only one to ten survive.[8] With the energy of the blessing, the creatures would become so abundant that they would be able to maintain their populations in the face of everyday threats, and still provide food for all who were hungry.

Biologist Cal Dewitt calls this first blessing, "the fruitfulness principle." While under ordinary circumstances a pair of creatures (without a blessing) would be expected to yield two offspring to replace the parents, with a blessing they could generate a surplus beyond the two. In economic terms the two "replacement" offspring correspond to "principle," while any additional offspring represent "interest." The blessing insures that the "principle" will always be preserved even if the "interest" is spent. This system provides the key to the sustainability of the creatures.

The medieval Jewish philosophers specifically addressed the twin notions of blessing and sustainability. They said that sustainability is a function of God's love or providence. God loves every species of creature and by this love, the creatures would never cease. "No species would ever become extinct."[9]

To some degree it appears the blessing worked, at least for the fish. The fish evolved in the Cambrian Period when it appears that new phyla and classes of sea animals came forth at a rate that has not been matched since.[10] Even today more animals abound in water than on land. The fertility of the fish is so great as to have become proverbial. The Hebrew word for fish, *dag*, comes from *dagah*, to increase prolifically.

Today the creatures need the blessing for fruitfulness and abundance more than ever. Frightening numbers of species are disappearing at staggering rates. Before the 1960s, the loss of species was due in large part to hunters, hungry for fresh game to eat, exotic feathers and skins to sell, and majestic antlered heads to mount in their lodges.

Now, with hunting in large part outlawed or contained, habitat destruction, the obliteration of entire ecosystems, is the greatest threat to all creatures. Since many animals have co-evolved in relation to particular species or places—beaks designed for particular kinds of foods, insects designed to pollinate particular flowers, behaviors hardwired to reproduce in a particular place—they can't just start looking for new apartments when their homes are destroyed; their anatomy or their wiring won't allow it. Salmon, for example, must return to their place of birth in order to reproduce. Now that most streams have been dammed or diverted, and only two hundred of the once six thousand miles of good salmon streams are left in California's Central Valley, salmon have become an endangered species.[11]

God designed the creation to be fruitful. The blessing promised a vast number of progeny, which could make up for any foreseeable losses. Yet God probably could not imagine that we would destroy habitats so completely that forty to one hundred species of animals and plants would be lost every day.

"We are living off the natural capital of the planet, the principal and not the interest," wrote David Brower.[12] God's impeccable design cannot ensure the perpetuation of life on earth if humanity wantonly intervenes and interferes with the design.

❧

And there was evening and there was morning, a fifth day. (1.23)

Va-yehi-erev va-yehi-voker yom chamishi.

❧

PEOPLE IN MOTION

With the completion of the fifth day comes a paradigm shift. While day three is the story of settledness, of plants that are rooted in the ground, day five is the story of movement, of animals traveling vast distances. Flying creatures and swimming creatures, the first moving creatures, are adapted for immense journeys. Their travel is not a choice; it is a necessity born of their chemistry. Migration is as basic to their livelihood as eating is. Without their voyages, these creatures could not reproduce and the species would become extinct.

One year I was running a wilderness trip on the Rogue River at the same time that thousands of salmon were making the return trip upriver enroute to the river's headwaters. I watched these sleek creatures swimming recklessly against the current, catapulting themselves through the air up twelve-foot drops, falling back in the water, tumbling downstream, and trying over again, all because of a fervent need to get to the one spot in the world where they could reproduce. The trip seemed so unlikely, so impossible.

Witnessing the salmon, I could feel the pull that a sacred place, a place of origins, has on its creatures. As they would make their way home, I felt more confident that so would I.

I am hungry for this feeling, this call to the open road, leading God-knows-where. I've often wondered if people need occasional treks in the open air to reorient their lives just like winged and water creatures do. Bruce Chatwin wrote in his book *The Songlines:*

> Natural Selection has designed us—from the structure of our brain-cells to the structure of our big toe—for a career of seasonal journeys on foot through the blistering land of thornscrub or desert.[13]

Chatwin maintained that the hunger to travel, the need for adventure, is innate, programmed into our anatomy; we can't escape it. An adventure brings refreshment and vigor to body, mind, and soul. The soul delights in uncertainty, the mind expands with new perspectives, and the body savors the exercise of its limbs. The ancients said that only the creatures that move have a soul and Genesis uses the word *nefesh*/soul in reference to various moving creatures. In turn, perhaps, movement is the way to a soulful life.

This is not to say we need to abandon our settled lives and become nomads. A rooted life (we recognize on day three) is critical to our homes, our communities, and our place, to all of our relationships. But we can get too settled, complacent, fixed in our ways and enslaved to owning things. We can sit ourselves into a stupor, into conformity, becoming pawns of the society. The Jewish commentator Sfat Emet says that our greatest enemy is torpor and habituation. Dwelling in cities that revolve around people and human needs, we can take our own accomplishments too seriously and become too full of ourselves.

Periodic journeys, especially journeys by foot, can pull us out from our psychological bonds, out from the world of human contrivances, and propel us forward in our lives. Journeying to wilderness or nature and seeing places and creatures outside of our ordinary reality can give us a perspective on our own place.

Most religions recognize the natural rhythm of staying home and taking to the road, of holding on and letting go. Muslims still walk to Mecca or Medina, Christians once walked to Canterbury, and ancient Jews walked to the Temple in Jerusalem on the *shalosh regalim*, the three on-foot days (pilgrimage holidays): Succot, Passover, and Shavuot (Pentecost).

Indeed most of the five books of the Hebrew Bible are dedicated to the story of the Israelite journey. The people had to be led on an epic trek through mountain and desert before they were actually able to settle in one place.

The point of this journey was never the destination—it was the journey itself. When the Israelites left Egypt, God did not lead them by the land of the Philistines or along the Mediterranean coast, either of which would have been easier and more direct. Instead God took them along the long, tortuous southern route.[14] A midrash says that God specifically decided against the northern route because it was shorter and less demanding. Ultimately it would take forty years of walking for the Israelites to shake loose and free themselves from the arrogance and greed that characterized their settled lives.

The Israelites learned many potent lessons in their wanderings. Stripped of their physical baggage and their financial status, they could actually experience the futility of acquiring things. The bigger the load, the greater the burden. On the road, less is more.

This lesson was made all the more transparent through the manna, which was sprinkled from the heavens each day for the Israelites to eat. They could eat as much as they wanted, but if they tried to save any, it would rot. The idea that everything in excess of what is necessary will only putrefy and decay is a powerful ecological one. A nomadic life was, by its very nature, ecologically sound—the Israelites practiced simple living as a matter of survival.

Journeying in the wilderness, subjected to the throws of uncertainty—not knowing where they were going and where the next meal would come from—the Israelites would learn to rely on a Power greater than themselves and become humble enough to finally receive the land of Israel. The physical setting of the wilderness itself clearly encouraged the Israelites' growth. Amidst the grandeur of the mountains and the wide expanse of the desert, they could discover the majesty of God's creation in light of their own relative smallness.

The spiritual journey and the humility it engenders has always provided people a doorway into their deeper selves. On the journey, away from the roles, responsibilities, and conventions of society, one has the space and the peace of mind to know oneself more deeply. Abraham was instructed by God to "walk the length and breadth of the land." Jacob, Joseph, Moses, and David, as well as many Israelite prophets, grew stronger and braver, able to cope with adversity through their years of wandering in the wilderness. More mature and wiser for their experience, they would return to their tribe, able to rise to the rigorous challenge of leading a whole people.

I imagine we can all benefit by balancing our settled lives with regular treks in the great outdoors. It's auspicious to time our journeys with the *shalosh regalim*, the three on-foot days or pilgrimage festivals: Succot, the fall harvest, Passover, the spring new year, and Shavuot, the spring harvest. The Bible prescribes making trips to Jerusalem on these occasions to "see and be seen" before God in the Holy Temple.[15]

6

LAND ANIMALS AND HUMANS

THE SIXTH DAY

And God said, "Let the earth bring forth a
living soul after its kind: cattle and creeper and wild
beast of the earth after its kind." And it was so.

And God made the wild beast of the earth
after its kind, and the cattle after its kind and every
creeper of the earth after its kind.
And God saw that it was good.

And God said, "Let us make adam
in our image, after our likeness, and let them have
dominion over the fish of the sea and the flyer
of the heaven and the cattle and all the earth and
every creeper that creeps on the earth."

And God created the adam *in God's own image;*
in the image of God, God created him, male and female
God created them.

And God blessed them and God said to them,
"Be fruitful and multiply and replenish the earth and
master it, and have dominion over the fish of the sea
and the flyer of the heaven, and every live creature
that creeps on the earth."

And God said, "See, I have given you
every grass bearing seed that is upon the face of
all the earth, and every tree that bears fruit,
seeding seed; it shall be yours for food.

And to every beast of the earth and to every flyer
of the heaven and to every creeper on the earth that
has a living soul, every green grass for food."
And it was so.

And God saw everything that God had made
and look! it was very good. And there was evening
and there was morning, the sixth day.

ﬞﮧﮧﮧﮧ

And God said, "Let the earth bring forth a living soul after its kind:
cattle and creeper and **wild beast** of the earth after its kind."
And it was so. (1.24)

Va-yomer Elohim totzai ha-aretz nefesh chayah le-minah
behaimah *va-remes ve-***chayto-eretz** *le-minah.*
Va-yehi khain.

ﬞﮧﮧﮧﮧ

THE CALL OF THE WILD

One might assume from the orderliness of the creation story and
the language: "God said," "God made," and "God saw" that God
stands outside the creation managing and ordering everything, but
God also grows the world from inside. God is the spontaneous energy that sparks life, the wild, enigmatic, interior aspect of all being.
God is simultaneously creator, owner, and keeper of the creatures,
and the divine force within each animal.

On the sixth day, God manifests in both the orderly and the
wild. God creates two primary categories of animals: the tame,
behaimah/cattle, and the wild, *chayto aretz*. The rabbis commented
that while *behaimah*/cattle eat only plant food and are domesticated
and cared for by people, the *chayto aretz* are largely carnivorous and
will not subordinate themselves to human rule.[1] And while cattle
live on domesticated land, wild animals need wilderness.

I had always dreamed of seeing wild animals in their natural environment, and when I was nineteen, I planned a two-week trek in the
Trinity Alps in northern California with my friends Mark and
George. Having never been in a "wilderness" before, the very term
was evocative for me, conjuring up images of a host of creatures,
wild and mysterious in their native habitat. "Backpacking" in the

"back" country, we would be utterly remote. I assumed that each day in wilderness would bring us further and further from civilization, and deeper and deeper into some primeval forest inhabited by fox or bear. I was eager to be scared.

In preparation for the journey we spent countless hours pouring over maps, studying our Petersen's guides to flora and fauna, and joking about all the creatures we hoped we could meet there. So when we finally arrived in the "Alps," I was disappointed because we didn't see any big game at all. The largest wild animal we encountered was a snake. My fantasies were further dispelled as we ran into all too many tame animals—human creatures—including neighbors from Berkeley.

Part of the reason we didn't see any wild creatures had to do with my naïve expectations. Most of the larger wild animals are nocturnal and would be in their lairs or dens sleeping during daytime hours while we were up and about. But even more important, many of the animals that had once inhabited these lands had been hunted out of existence or could not find enough food to survive in such a restricted island of wilderness. My experience gave me a glimpse of the profound losses we incur by civilizing nature.

Wild animals are critical, not just in and of themselves, but for the genetic potential that they embody. Wildness—untouched by human hands—is the closest thing to godliness, to the source of life. The literal meaning of *chayato aretz*, usually translated as wild animals, is "life of the earth." Wildness is synonymous with life, and the source of life. Like nature's libraries or memory banks, wild creatures store the instructions for life's extraordinary variety.

Wild animals cannot live without wild places, and the animals, in turn, sustain the places and ecosystems of which they are a part. The larger the wild creature, the larger the territory it needs to find enough food to stay alive. If a large wild animal population remains intact, so will the other populations that inhabit the same habitat.

Until the 1930s scientists believed that the large wild animals like wolves, mountain lions, and jaguars, who sit at the top of the food chain, exerted little influence on the overall functioning of the natural system. The National Park Service viewed gray wolves and mountain lions as pests that threatened tourists, and exterminated them from Yellowstone and other parks. Even Aldo Leopold, the godfather of the modern environmental movement, supported the eradication of gray wolves in national parks until, in his later years he came to recognize the dynamics of ecological systems.

Now many of us who live in cities and suburbs know more than we'd like to about the value large wild animals afford our ecosystems. Since the wolves and coyotes have been hunted out of many semi-urban locations throughout the east, our woods and backyards have become overrun with deer. They feast on new growth of the forest understory, thereby hindering the regeneration of trees and shrubs, changing the composition of the forest, and weakening the entire ecosystem. Were the wolves and mountain lions to be reintroduced here, they would scatter the deer and eat them, and the forest could return to its natural composition of species and pattern of succession.

Large wild animals, then, are indicators of a balanced ecosystem; they help maintain the genetic diversity on which we all depend.

THE FEAR OF THE WILD

In many ancient communities, people understood that wildness contributed to the health of the larger whole and included a place for it in their consciousness and their maps. The Bible prescribed an area for the camp organized in circular fashion with the tabernacle in the center and tents all around it, and beyond that, a wilderness, off limits to people.

Puritan New England was similarly designed in concentric circles with the Congregational church and village green in the center surrounded by houses of the community members. Next was a ring of common fields for livestock, then the estates of the wealthy landowners, and beyond that were farms that provided crops for the town. The outermost ring was considered wilderness, designated for swamps and waste heaps. Wilderness was shunned and feared but it was also mapped. In other words, even though they were afraid of it, the people recognized that wilderness around the periphery of the town formed a container that helped give meaning to the ordered life within.

The value of wildness, essential to God's design, is lost on us moderns, as we so enthusiastically domesticate every last inch of our world, damming rivers, clear cutting forests, reconfiguring genes, and lighting up the night in the name of civilization. Today we are witnessing, indeed participating in, the greatest mass extinction since the disappearance of the dinosaurs brought about by the end of the Cretaceous Period sixty-five million years ago. The world's leading ecologists warn that one third of all species living may become extinct in the next twenty to thirty years, and that by the middle of the twenty-first century the only large mammals remaining will be those that people protect.

It's not just a sense of greed that drives us to domesticate nature and treat it as resource for our consumption. It is also a reaction to fear. Nature comes in the form of frightening beasts, floods, disease, hurricanes, and earthquakes as well as sunshine and rain. Nature's way, God's way, is utterly beyond our control; it is simultaneously a benevolent and fearsome presence.

In our society we are not encouraged to meet our fears head on; we tend to control whatever frightens us. So we domesticate wild lands and exterminate wild beasts. But there are always consequences when we oppose nature. Every action generates a reaction: when we wage war against bacteria, penicillin-resistant strains emerge; when we build dams to control possible floods, bigger waters spill over the flood walls; when we try to control the natural cycle of fires, larger fires burn out of control.

As we strive to domesticate the outer wildness, we unwittingly clamp down on our inner wildness. In doing so, we lose our connection with our instincts and creativity and with a wild and mysterious God. We lose our ability to find answers to problems within, to learn from the body's wisdom, and to be at peace with the unknown.

The psychiatrist Carl Jung said that, try as we will to exorcise the outer wild demons, they will take up residence elsewhere—namely in the deepest reaches of our psyches. He believed that anxiety disorders, neuroses, drug problems, alcoholism, high divorce rates, and restlessness result from our separation from nature and particularly our separation from our own wild nature; they result when we try too hard to tame our own wildness.

Jung suggested that we need to find our way "back to nature." By this he meant, not just to Rousseau's external nature, but, also to our own internal nature, our emotions: our fears and joys, our creativity, our intuitions, the wild within.[2] Rather than controlling and putting a lid on our fears, our wildness, and the feelings we can't understand, we will grow healthier as we get to know these less pretty aspects of our selves.

It is not surprising then that the Bible abounds with frightening, indeed terrifying, images of God. The more we fear nature, the greater our sense of awe, the more we can recognize the Divine in it. Indeed these two words, fear and awe, derive from the same Hebrew root, *yrh*.

The ancients regularly confronted their terrors concretely by coming together collectively and publicly to recite prayers and incantations and perform sacrifices. Such rituals performed a vital societal and personal function. Individuals in these societies developed a respect for forces larger than themselves and acknowledged their fears while keeping them at bay, away from the holy ground of their inner sanctum.

Today we need to welcome the wild back into our lives and our environments. We must find ways to keep our fears from ruling us so that we don't end up ruling nature. We need to let our wild nature heal us as we allow nature to heal.

❋

And God made the wild beast of the earth after its kind, and
the cattle after its kind and every creeper of the earth after its kind.
And God **saw** that it was **good**. (1.25)

Va-ya'as Elohim et-chayat ha-aretz le-minah ve-et
ha-behaimah le-minah ve-et kol-remes ha-adamah le-minaihu.
*Va-**yar** Elohim ki-**tov**.*

SEEING THE GOODNESS OF NATURE

On this day as on every other, God "saw" that the creations were
"good." The world was created to be seen. Simply by observing
creation, we can know what "good" actually means.

When we make a point of looking, we find a staggering array
of creatures in countless hues, shapes, and designs—a feast for the
eyes: more beauty, more adventure in form than we humans could
even dream of. The Creator is the ultimate artist, playing with colors and shapes and arriving at marvelous effects: from spiraling
antlers to striped zebra skins to iridescent peacock feathers.

At first glance it may seem frivolous to interpret the stunning
array of the colors, patterns, and forms of creation as significant.
Many of us approach life like scientists, analyzing, delving beneath
the surface, yet sometimes overlooking the simple truth that lies
right before our eyes. We dismiss the exterior surface of a creature,
arguing that the outside of a creature is merely a cover for the "vital
organs," the heart and brain. We assume that no matter how excep-
tional the skin, the feathers or the fur, they're nothing more than a
fortuitous byproduct of some other bodily function. We think of
the world in terms of its utility and practicality, not its beauty.

But when we compare the visual effects of the "outside" of an
animal (particularly a higher animal) to the "inside," it becomes obvious that the skin is more than just a bag holding the internal organs together. While the outside of a creature is often pleasing or

striking, the insides are usually drab and plain: one creature's insides are indistinguishable from the next. Only an expert can differentiate a lion's guts from a tiger's, but even a child can tell a lion from a tiger. A great mystery exists beyond function in the forms themselves.

That the outside is meant to be seen can be further observed in the symmetrical design of most creatures. Animals, including people, are bilaterally symmetrical; right and left sides mirror each other almost perfectly. Symmetry invites our gaze. Not so the internal organs. We have matching right and left lungs and kidneys, but the heart is off to the left, and the liver to the right, and the pancreas spans both sides, and the digestive system is one long tube folded over and over in on itself. The outward appearance presented to the eye is clearly formed according to different laws than the internal organs that are hidden from view.

Visible forms make an impression on us, and are as much a part of the Creator's design as the functional dimensions of the creations. Just as sounds are meant to be heard and foods are meant to be tasted, visual effects are meant to be seen. The more we exercise our eyes and all of our senses—the organs of reception—the more we receive. The Jewish philosopher Bahya Ibn Pakuda said we must observe all of God's creations, and meditate upon them, for the natural world is as much an expression of God's love as the Torah is.[3] Beauty, nature's ever-expanding palette of forms and colors, is the outer expression of the mystery of life. It invites our gaze and beckons us into relationship with creation and the Creator.

I am particularly sensitive to what I "see." Perhaps hypersensitive. Indeed it is this sensitivity, in part, that made an ecologist out of me. I have never been able to understand why people are willing to trade so much God-given beauty in the form of landscapes and the creatures that inhabit them for acres of malls and tract housing. It is as if a whole generation has dismissed the sense of sight.

Growing up, I got a subliminal message that the beauty of the world did not hold any particular value in Judaism. I was raised in a community that consumed and accumulated the artifacts of the natural world, but never actually paid too much attention to the nature of the products themselves. My home, the synagogue, and the homes of others I knew were all large, uninteresting buildings, devoid of art or craft or character. One's possessions were symbolic of status and success, indicators of rank in a pecking order. There was no real love of material here.

The Judaism I grew up with was cut off from the body, the senses, and nature. It was a disembodied Judaism, which elevated the word and cerebral activity, while diminishing the sensual.

In my adult exploration of Judaism, I often wondered if there was an ideology in Judaism—perhaps rooted in the prohibition against graven images—that leads to a discouraging of the visual. Rabbi Norman Lamm, a respected contemporary leader, argues that "hearing" is the superior sense. "Seeing," he says, "leads to idolatry; the worshipper creates an icon to represent what he saw." Lamm reinforces his position by citing the Catholic historian Theodore Roszak, who writes that Jews have "acquired an incomparable ear in exchange for surrendering their visual and tactile witness."[4]

There is no question that the Israelites had a refined sense of hearing. The people "heard" the voice of God at Sinai and most of the patriarchs and prophets were "called" to service. The central prayer of the Jewish liturgy commands us—"Hear, O Israel." Philosophers have asserted that whereas the Greeks thought with the eye, the Hebrews thought with the ear.

Hearing and speech are complementary faculties. Speech is the external expression of our inner words and thoughts. It is often the criteria by which we distinguish ourselves from, and claim superiority over, animals. A facility with words certainly characterizes the Jews, the people of the book. Perhaps the early rabbis were so preoccupied with listening and words that they paid less attention to the nonverbal ways of knowing, the knowing that comes through sight and the other senses.

While our ears enable us to perceive without an immediate physical presence, our eyes and other sensors—the tongue and the fingers—demand a direct experience of a material object. Hearing is more a function of time, while sight is a function of place. We hear sequentially, absorbing one message at a time, but we see all at once. Hearing allows us to perceive more easily the parts, while seeing provides the whole picture. Perhaps it follows that hearing leads to analytic thought and an abstracted reality, while seeing and the other senses lead to relational thought and a more concrete reality.

Hearing and seeing may be two necessary parts of a whole. Just as the character of light can only be fully understood through knowledge of both particles and waves, perhaps nature can only be fully understood through the integration of sight and hearing.

While attitudes that neglect sight and beauty—and in turn nature—and elevate speech and hearing do persist in Jewish culture, such attitudes are not grounded in the Torah or liturgy. The Torah, the Psalms, the Writings, and the Prophets are steeped in the sensual world and are replete with references to sight and the beauty of nature. Everywhere the images of nature are an invitation to contemplate the mystery of God.

I'm building this case for seeing, because I believe that at the heart of the environmental crisis is a perceptual problem. If we don't take sight seriously, then neither will we take the primary object of sight, nature, seriously. When we, as individuals or a culture, favor one type of knowing or one sense to the detriment of the others, our lives and the life of nature are the poorer for it. It's important to cultivate whatever senses we have neglected in order to create wholeness.

When I was leading wilderness river trips on the Klamath River in northern California, my coleaders and I tried to help people see the beauty of nature. This is not as simple as you might think. We bring our ideas, our thoughts, our words, with us wherever we go and this cultural baggage often gets in the way of seeing. Our traveling companions, even in the midst of wilderness, were not eager (or did not know how) to let go of their attachments, their radios and tape players, and their constant chatter.

So we instituted certain rituals to help break the grip that words hold on us. On each trip, we would take time out from our paddling for a silent hike to Ukinom Falls, an hour-long trek along Ukinom Creek. Without the distraction of speech, we could tune ourselves into a more visual and sensual reality.

This trip was not for the faint-hearted. The going demanded one's complete awareness and this was the point: to force ourselves to look. It was rattlesnake country. The path was narrow, windy, and steep, and the rocks were often slippery; we had to slow down enough to watch every step. At certain spots we needed to swim up the creek in order to recover the trail. By the time we reached the twenty-foot falls, we had been initiated into a different reality. We saw the water, roaring and tumbling over a steep precipice into a deep emerald pool carved of granite, but we saw more than that. We experienced a sense of oneness, a sense of intimacy with nature that was only possible because we had begun to see with "beginner's eyes."

On the sixth day as on every other, God looked out over creation and saw its goodness. According to Philo, "good" refers to proportion, harmony, and beauty. Nature, in its countless faces, is as much an expression of divine goodness as the Torah is, and it is incumbent upon us to bear witness to it and abide by its wisdom.

❧

And God said, "**Let us** make adam in **our** image, after **our** likeness,
and let them have dominion over the fish of the sea
and the flyer of the heaven
and the cattle and all the earth and every creeper
that creeps on the earth."(1.26)

*Va-yomer Elohim **naaseh** adam be-tzalm**ainu** kidmut**ainu***
ve-yirdu bi-degat ha-yam
u-ve-of ha-shamayim
u-va-behaimah u-ve-khol-ha-aretz u-ve khol-ha remes
ha-romais al-ha-aretz.

❧

HOW TO CREATE AN ADAM

God's final creation would be a joint endeavor, a partnership between God and someone/something else. God says, "Let us make the *adam* in our image, after our likeness." While the earlier verses only imply that God works with the various habitats to bring forth the creatures, here God explicitly requests others to participate in the design of the first human.

Who are the "others" God is talking to? Some rabbis suggest that God is talking with the angels: "God spoke to the angels: 'Let us make man! We ourselves will engage in his creation, not the water or earth!'"[5]

The Zohar, a Jewish mystical text, says that God is speaking with the four winds (of the four directions). The wind is as elemental to the creation of the *adam* as earth is. God took a clod of earth, breathed wind into it, and the human became a "living soul."

Nachmanides asserts that God is speaking with the earth.[6] The same earth that shaped the plants and animals would shape the adam, the human. The intimate relation between human, earth, and earthly creatures is rooted in the language itself. The *adam*, the human, was formed from *adamah*, the earth. And *dam*, blood, contains the soul and distinguishes the animal world from the plant world, while *adom*, red, is the color of earth and blood. According to Hebrew, the essence of humanity, animals, and earth is the same. English provides similar nuances. The words human, humus, humble, and humility all derive from the same root "hum," which means ground.

The Vilna Gaon suggests that God is addressing all the birds and beasts, inviting each to contribute its particular strength to the new human creature. God calls for might from the lion, cunning from the fox, and swiftness from the eagle.[7] Biologically speaking, the human creature does indeed draw on features from the rest of the animals. In the womb, the fetus progresses through various stages of development that recall the history of evolution. At one point, the human fetus even has gill pouches in the throat area resembling fish ancestors.

Even as the creatures helped to create the *adam*/human, they empowered the *adam* to rule over them. Perhaps they thought that the world would be too chaotic without a single species maintaining order. Trading a bit of freedom was a small price to pay for the possibility of harmony. (We, after all, choose individuals all the time to govern us.) The human, standing erect, head in the heaven, feet rooted in the earth, blending the earthly qualities of the lower world and the spiritual qualities of the upper world, appeared the obvious candidate to govern over all.

Chosen by the creatures to rule over them, the *adam's* job is to minister to all of creatures' needs. If the *adam* could act on behalf of both heaven and earth, he/she would be able to lift the earth and its creatures to greater heights. "His (the *adam's*) mastery is no enslavement or degradation," wrote Samson Raphael Hirsch, "but rather an . . . elevation of all earthly material into the sphere of free-willed . . . God-serving purposes."[8]

SUSTAINING CREATION

Ruling nature humanely does not mean that humanity must refrain from partaking of the produce of nature. God provided the plants and animals with a mechanism to reproduce themselves so that they would bear fruit abundantly in perpetuity. People could take of the surplus or the "interest"—the increase in produce beyond what was necessary to insure the next generation of plant or animal. Taking of the increase would not harm the creation or interfere with the Creator's design. Indeed, consuming the increase is part of the Creator's plan, and we are expected to delight in this. We don't need to starve ourselves of all worldly pleasures in order to save nature.

The Bible teaches us how we can feed and shelter ourselves while still insuring that there will be enough to sustain the creation forever.

> "If, along the road, you chance upon a bird's nest in a tree
> or on the ground, with fledglings or eggs in it and the
> mother is roosting there with the fledglings or the eggs, do

not take the mother together with her young. Let the mother go and take only the young in order that you may fare well and have a long life."[9]

The law is simultaneously concerned with providing for humanity, sustaining the species and alleviating suffering. If you snatch both the baby birds (or the eggs) and their mother, you could destroy an entire species. And if you took the mother, but left the eggs, the eggs would not hatch, or if they did, the young would probably die of hunger. But if you sent the mother away and took just the eggs, the mother would lay more eggs, and undoubtedly would not suffer terribly from the loss of her progeny (at least she would not witness the loss). Similarly, another law concerned with sustainability prohibits mating different species together because crossing different "kinds" produce sterile offspring, thereby denying a future for the species.[10]

For people to take only what they need (the increase/interest), without hoarding and depleting the parent stock or principle, demands constant forethought and consideration. We humans have an insatiable hunger for the produce of nature and feel entitled to it; it seems there is no end to our desire. Exercising discernment in all of our relations with the natural world appears to be humanity's greatest challenge in every generation.

❧

And God created the **adam** in God's own image; in the image of God, God created him, **male** and **female** God created **them**. (1.27)

*Va-yivra Elohim et ha-**adam** be-tzalmo be-tzelem Elohim bara oto **zakhur** u-**nekaiveh** bara **otam.***

❧

IN GOD'S IMAGE: A BALANCE OF MALE AND FEMALE

The *adam*, or human, described simultaneously as male, and male-and-female, is unique among the creatures. According to some rabbis, the first *adam* was androgynous, a melding of man and woman.

The one *adam* creature, formed in God's image, balances the qualities of both sexes and serves as the blueprint for all of humanity.

Other rabbis said that the *adam* is really two matching and separate creatures: Adam and Eve. Alone, Adam would have led a static and unchanging life. So God drew Eve out of Adam's side as a *kenegdo*, a "helpmeet" (translated by Robert Alter as "lifesaver"), the one who would help him, meet him face to face, and challenge him so he would grow and change.

Genesis 1:27 makes a point of the equality of male and female. However we understand this cryptic language, man and woman were created equally and directly by God, in God's likeness. Man and woman have an equal share in the divine charge.

Regardless of the biblical prescription, men have assumed superiority over women for thousands of years. Our Western civilization has been molded by patriarchy and is scarred by innumerable wars and violence resulting from unchecked male aggression.

Feminists have called attention to the ways in which patriarchy has been oppressive and abusive of the feminine—both of feminine characteristics and of women themselves. Ecofeminists, among others, claim that male aggressiveness has also led to the rape of nature.

While on the one hand, our culture has been framed by an aggressive patriarchy, on the other, I personally felt very little male influence in my community growing up. In my own family and many of the immigrant families I knew, the mother appeared dominant and the father powerless. I grew up in a matriarchy in which the men didn't stand up for themselves.

By the time I was in college in the early 1970s, at the height of the women's movement, men were the object of a tremendous amount of female anger. Many feminists wanted men to be softer and more sensitive, more expressive, more relational, less willful, more like women. Not me. As far as I was concerned our culture was already too soft, too domesticated, too obsessed with comforts and convenience. I was looking for men who loved the wild, the chaotic, the unknown.

I felt empathy for men. They seemed like the ultimate victims of the patriarchy. Even though women have suffered career discrimination and lower salaries, women have generally been better able to develop their inner lives. Women are more likely to know themselves, be comfortable in their bodies, trust their intuition, and be in touch with their feelings than men, who often don't have much of a life outside of their jobs. Bound to societal expectations, men hide out in their work. Their identities and happiness seems inextricably tied up with what they own, or what they can physically show for themselves. Many have lost touch with their heart's desire, their adventure lust, their sense of honor. They are, to use the language of Thoreau, "living lives of quiet desperation."

Asking for men to become softer and less aggressive never seemed like the right strategy to me. As the Jungians teach, if we don't acknowledge the darker aspects of our selves and our culture, they will turn up to haunt us when we least expect it. We may erase the warriors from our prayer books—some Christians have excised the "Battle Hymn of the Republic" and some Jews have deleted "Moses' Song at the Sea"—and forbid our children from playing with toy guns, but the aggressive energy shows up in a twisted form somewhere else, because we cannot evade these primal mythic energies.

While aggressiveness is the attribute of the warrior that is responsible for destruction, it is also the attribute responsible for energizing, initiating, and pushing forward. Aggressiveness motivates people to move out of defensive holding patterns, laziness, and sloth, into stronger, more offensive postures, ready to meet the world and take on the challenges that life presents.

The warrior trains his body and hones his mind so he is alert, clear-headed, and prepared to make instantaneous strategic and tactical decisions. He is brave, knows his limits, has an unbeatable spirit, and is willing to sacrifice in order to achieve his dreams. The mature warrior is loyal to something larger than himself, be it freedom, nature, justice, or God. He chooses his battles carefully and fights the ones that must be fought; he destroys that which needs destruction—corruption, greed, oppression, corporate hierarchies, environmental injustices, conspicuous consumption, unhealthy job situations. All of these situations waste time and energy and keep us lost and preoccupied in our small selves, detracting us from living fuller lives of giving and goodness.

According to Jewish mysticism, the male energy centers (similar to chakras) are located on the right side of the body—right brain, right arm, right leg—and the female centers are on the corresponding parts of the left. The Jewish mystical map of male and female typologies shares some, but not all, characteristics with eastern spiritual systems in which female or yin energy is conceived of as empty, passive, receptive, unconscious, and intuitive; while male or yang energy is conceived of as filling, active, assertive, conscious, and reasoning. Even though certain qualities are described as male and others as female, this does not mean that men are governed by the male energy centers and women the female ones. All energy centers are active to differing degrees in different people. The kabbalistic map of consciousness is sketched below:

female—being, receiving qualities	male—doing, reaching qualities
binah—understanding	chokhmah—wisdom
gevurah—boundaries	chesed—love, expansiveness
hod—humility, splendor	netzach—victory, warrior

In the kabbalistic model, *netzach*/warrior energy does not exist in isolation; it is bound up with the other male qualities of *chesed*/unbounded love and *chokhmah*/wisdom. The connection of *netzach*/aggressiveness to *chesed*/love gives the warrior compassion and a sense of connectedness with everything. It brings him into relation with other people in service to a higher good. The connection of *netzach* to *chokhmah*/wisdom gives the warrior the clarity and ability to assess between right and wrong and to know which battles are worth fighting. The true warrior is no thoughtless, heartless savage.

This model of the masculine stands in opposition to the one espoused by some who submit that males are hard-wired to abuse, and that love, relatedness, and gentleness are distinctly feminine traits.

We need that warrior energy today to carry on a campaign for the honor of the earth and its people. We need men and women who can stand up and fight the battles that need to be fought, who can take leadership, who are not afraid to express a different view.

The female qualities, of course, are equally essential to the development of both healthy women and men. *Hod*, the female energy center that balances *netzach*, the warrior energy, is associated with humility and splendor. The word *hod* is related to the Hebrew word for thank; *hod* is the ability to express gratitude. When we are in touch with gratitude, we recognize that all of creation is a gift and we can experience the splendor of the world. Gratitude is the first and most important step to a fulfilled life and it lays the foundation for a creation ethic. We will never take care of creation effectively unless we cultivate an appreciation of it.

Gevurah, the female energy center that balances *chesed*/unbounded love, is associated with boundaries and limits. For us to know who we are, as distinct from others, we must have limits—we must say "no" to what we are not. *Gevurah* gives character and strength and enables us to stand up for ourselves. It also encourages us to limit ourselves and our excesses. It allows us to know when enough is enough so that we do not take more than we need.

Healthy individuals balance the male and female sides. *Netzach*/warrior energy, symbolized by the right hip, must be tempered by *hod*/humility, the left hip. Metaphorically speaking, without this balance, we cannot walk. We cannot move forward. Too much *hod*/humility without enough *netzach*/warrior energy, and we are hesitant and self-effacing. Too much *netzach*/warrior without enough *hod*/humility, and we are too full of our selves.

Similarly, *chesed*, which means limitless love or expansiveness and is symbolized by the right arm, must be balanced by *gevurah*/limits, or the left arm. While *chesed* means love, it also means "to drain." Too much unbounded love/*chesed* without a container/*gevurah* to hold it, and all the good intentions of chesed just evaporate or leak away. On the other hand, too much *gevurah*/ boundaries, and we strangle the flow of love. We need both. *Chesed* is the right arm gathering in the good; *gevurah* is the left arm warding off the bad.

Finally, *binah*/intuition must be balanced with *chokhmah*. *Chokhmah* is the reaching kind of intelligence, the ability to reason, analyze, and think abstractly, while *binah* is the receiving kind of intelligence, the understanding that results from relationships and experience in the world.

It is vital that we recognize the forces alive within each of us, so that we can be more effective people, at peace with ourselves and our inherent contradictions, and better able to enjoy our lives and serve. The balance and health we want for the world requires that we create balances and health in ourselves.

And God **blessed** them and God said to them,
"Be **fruitful** and **multiply** and **replenish** the earth
and **master** it, and **have dominion** over the fish of the sea and the flyer
of the heaven, and every live creature that creeps on the earth." (1.28)

Va-**yivarekh** otam Elohim va-yomer lahem Elohim
Peru u-**revu** u-**milu** et-ha-aretz
ve-**khiveshuha** u-**redu** bi-degat ha-yam u-ve-of
ha-shamayim u-ve-khol chayah ha-romeset al-ha-aretz.

THE HUMAN PLACE IN NATURE

In 1967, historian Lynn White argued in a now famous essay in *Science* magazine that the Bible gave humanity a mandate to exploit nature when it empowered the *adam*/human to "master the earth," and "have dominion over" it.[11] Many environmentalists and theologians are still haggling over White's thesis even after hundreds of articles and books have tackled the topic over the last thirty years.[12]

In my environmental studies courses at U.C. Berkeley in the early 1970s, we read White's article and were taught that the theology of the Bible laid the ideological roots for the contemporary environmental crisis. I naïvely accepted this idea, having no real knowledge of the Bible and no positive experience of religion. It was comforting to find a scapegoat to blame for society's problems, and religion has always been an easy target.

White's interpretation of Genesis had enormous ramifications on a whole generation of environmentalists and their students. I still encounter some who challenge my work, insisting that Judaism couldn't possibly have ecological integrity because "the Bible encourages people to control nature." They shun organized religion, claiming that it is the source of the environmental problem.

It is conceivable that people who have little experience reading the Bible could examine this verse and decide that the language of "dominion" and "mastery over nature" is anti-ecological. But a verse is not a collection of words, just like nature is not a collection of plants and animals. Extracting a word or verse out of its context is like removing a tree from its habitat, taking it from the soil, the weather, and all the creatures with which it lives in total interdependence. It would be impossible to really know the tree outside of its relationships. It's no different with the Bible. When you read the Bible, you have to consider the derivation of the words under consideration, the meaning of the neighboring words and verses, the message of the Bible as a whole, the context in which it was written, and how others have understood the verse throughout its three-thousand-year history.[13]

The context of "dominion" in this verse is a blessing/*bracha*, a divine act of love. While God blessed the birds and fishes with fertility, God blessed humanity with both fertility and authority over nature. In more abstract terms the fish receive a blessing in a horizontal dimension while the *adam* is blessed in both horizontal and vertical dimensions. Like the animals the *adam* is called to multiply and spread over the earth, but unlike the animals, he stands upright as God's representative, overseeing all the animals and the plants.[14]

Dominion is an awesome responsibility. The psalmist captures the sense of undeserved honor that humanity holds:

> What are human beings that You are mindful of them
> Mortals that You care for them?
> You have made them a little lower than God,
> And crowned them with glory and honor.
> You have given them dominion over the works of Your hands,
> You have put all things under their feet,
> all sheep and oxen and also the beasts of the field the
>   birds of the air
> and the fish of the sea, whatever passes along the paths
>   of the sea.[15]

As a blessing, responsibility for creation is a gift. According to anthropologist William Hyde, the recipients of a gift become custodians of the gift. The creation is a sacred trust and dominion is the most profound privilege.

It is necessary to remember the context of blessing as we examine the so-called "accused" words, *kvs*, "master," and *rdh*, "have dominion over." It is also important to remember that Hebrew is a more symbolic, multilayered, and vague language than English— any single word root can have multiple meanings and often a word and its opposite will share the same word root. According to Bible scholar Norbert Samuelson, both *kvs*/master and *rdh*/have dominion over, appear in these particular grammatical forms here and nowhere else in the Bible, so translating them is not a cut and dried affair. The root of the Hebrew word for mastery, *kvs*, comes from the Aramaic "to tread down" or "make a path." In the book of Zechariah, the root *kvs* is interchangeable with the root *akl*, the word for "eat." Although *kvs* is often translated as "subdue" or "master," it appears to have agricultural implications.[16]

The root of the Hebrew word for "have dominion over," *rdh*, generally refers to the "rule over subjects." In a play on the word *rdh*, Rashi, the foremost medieval rabbinic commentator, explains that if we consciously embody God's image and rule with wisdom and compassion, we will rise above the animals and preside over, *rdh*, them, insuring a life of harmony on earth. However if we are oblivious to our power and deny our responsibility to creation, we will *yrd*, sink below the level of the animals and bring ruin to ourselves and the world.[17] If we twist the blessing to further our own ends, the blessing becomes a curse. The choice is ours.

As I was writing my book, I had long discussions with environmentalists and feminists who urged me to substitute a less "offensive" word for the word "dominion," the traditional translation of *rdh*. They argued that "dominion" carries the negative connotations of control and domination. I considered what they said, and pondered the nuances of other words like "govern" or "preside over" (one feminist suggested "have provenance over"). I decided that while these words are less offensive, they are also less inspired; they do not carry the sense of dignity and nobility captured by "dominion"; they do not reflect the commitment to take responsibility for something much larger than oneself.

Like the Hebrew *rdh*, "dominion" implies two sides: graciousness and domination. Dominion, like money, is not in itself bad; it all depends on how we exercise it. As Rashi said, we can recognize our responsibility to nature and rise to the occasion to create an extraordinary world, or we can deny our responsibility and sink to our basest instincts (dominate nature) and destroy the world. Such is the human condition. It is time that we understand our conflicting tendencies and deal with them, rather than deny their existence.[18]

Humanity's role is to tend the garden, not to possess it; to "guard it and keep it,"[19] not to exploit it; to pass it on as a sacred trust. Even though we are given the authority to have dominion over the earth and its creatures, we are never allowed to own it, just like we can't own the waters or the air. "The land cannot be sold in perpetuity."[20] The land is the commons and it belongs to everyone equally and jointly. In the biblical system, private property does not even exist because God owns the land and everything in it. (When the state of Israel was established, the Jewish National Fund took responsibility for the management of the land—with an original intention to insure its perpetuity.)

The blessing of mastery over the earth calls us to exercise compassion and wisdom in our relationship with nature so that the creation will keep on creating for future generations. We use nature every day in every thing we do; nature provides our food, shelter, clothing, energy, electricity, coal, gas. "Mastering" nature involves determining how much land and which animals should be designated for human use and the development of civilization, and what should remain untouched.

According to Sadia Gaon in the eleventh century, "mastery" of nature meant harnessing the energy of water and wind and fire, cultivating the soil for food, using plants for medicines, fashioning utensils for eating and writing, and developing tools for agricultural work, carpentry and weaving. It meant the beginning of art, science, agriculture, metallurgy, architecture, music, technology, animal husbandry, land use planning, and urban development.[21]

That the power is in humanity's hands is clearly a risk for all of creation. Indeed the rabbis question why God created humanity, with the capacity to do evil, in the first place. Some of them figured that humanity would only destroy itself and the world. But our ability to choose between good and bad is what makes us human. Free choice is what distinguishes us from animals, who follow their instinct, and angels, who have no will of their own and act entirely on God's decrees. It is up to us to determine if we will make of ourselves a blessing or a curse. To rule nature with wisdom and compassion is our greatest challenge, our growth edge. It demands that we understand ourselves and guard against our own excesses and extremes; it demands a constant level of heightened awareness.

✦

One of the pleasures of grappling with a biblical text is that one can always find new meanings in it. Over the years as I've turned this verse over and over, I've discovered a psycho-spiritual nuance. The complementary pair of blessings, "fertility" and "mastery," can be understood as blessings for "love" and "work." Fertility implies love, creativity, and being; mastery implies work, strength, and doing.

For most of us love and work are the two dimensions that define our lives; for Freud they set the criteria for a healthy life. The complementary pair, love and work, take other forms such as being and doing, sex and power. God blesses us with the ability to experience both. Yet our contemporary worldview attributes more value to our dominating side, to work, than to our fertile side, to love. It's important to temper our dominating tendencies with our fertile, creative ones, and to remember that mastery over the earth is a sacred act just like love is. They both invite the divine in us.

❧

And God said, "See, I have given you **every grass seeding seed** that is on the face of all the earth and **every tree bearing fruit, seeding seed;** it shall be yours for food. (1.29)

*Va-yomer Elohim hinaih natati lakhem et-kol-**aisev zoraia zera** asher al-penai khol ha-aretz ve-et kol **ha-aitz asher-bo peri-aitz zoraia zara** lakhem yihyeh le-akhlah.*

❧

FOOD FOR PEOPLE

The way in which we are invited to exercise dominion over the earth is by eating its produce. Through the act of eating, we incorporate the body and the energy of another, and become indelibly woven together with it into the tapestry of creation.

While we are given dominion over the creatures, when it comes to eating, our dominion is restricted; we can only eat plants. And even here we are limited. God bids us to enjoy the fruits of the trees and the fruits of the grasses: the wheat berry, the grains of rye, the kernels of corn, but we are not offered, nor are we equipped to eat, the grasses themselves or the trees.

Still the fruits of the grasses and the trees alone offer an astonishing variety—more tastes, flavors, shapes, textures, colors, and smells than we could ever dream of. It is our good fortune that God provided us with so many kinds of delicious fruits to eat. Simply by eating, we enter a magical doorway into the pleasure and delight of the natural world.

Some vegetarians use this biblical verse to substantiate their claim that we are "meant" to eat only plants.[22] I recently read an article that said that our facial muscles are specifically adapted to help us grind and chew vegetables. If we were "meant" to be meat-eaters, the advocates for vegetarianism say, we wouldn't have such sophisticated facial apparatus. Carnivores don't have such fancy facial muscles because they don't chew (they also don't smile or grimace); they use their canines to tear food and they can swallow big chunks of meat whole because their enormous stomachs do most of the digesting, not their mouths.

Numerous other bits of anatomical evidence point to the fact that we are naturally adapted to the work of digesting fruits and grains: our teeth are adapted for mashing up food, our saliva for breaking it down and our small intestine is relatively long (ten to eleven times our body length as compared to carnivores, whose small intestine is only about four times their body length) enabling us to digest grains and roughage.

This evidence still does not convince me that I am supposed to eat just plants. My experience teaches me otherwise. I love vegetables and my diet consists largely of greens and herbs, but I am always grateful for special opportunities for eating meat.

I became a vegetarian as a teenager when a friend and I decided that we wanted to eat lower on the food chain. Besides, we had had just one too many meals of chipped beef on toast in the dormitory dining hall. We would scrounge around the room after lunch, table by table, looking for remains of mashed potatoes, relish, and ketchup, the only foods that seemed to fit the criteria of our diet.

Even with this bizarre concoction of foods as my entrée to vegetarianism, I remained a vegetarian for about fourteen years, although happily, I expanded my diet beyond the meager pickings of my adolescence. I learned more creative cookery on our vegetarian wilderness trips. We found many ways to get enough protein; we added tofu to everything including desert—tofu cheesecake cooked in a Dutch oven became a company staple.

But my vegetarian days were numbered. During that stretch of my life I was often tired, hungry, and unsatisfied. I needed to graze between meals. Not having the presence of mind to do "food combining" or the patience to cook more than the simplest of meals, I was unhealthy as a vegetarian. I'm sure that vegetarianism is right for many people today and would have been the ideal diet in the Garden of Eden where life was relatively stress free, but given the sometimes frenetic pace of my life, I feel better and function better when I supplement my diet of grains, greens, and dairy products with chicken, meat, and fish.

Lately, I've come to the conclusion that how I eat is more important than what I eat. My eating habits leave a lot to be desired. It is rare for me to remember where my food comes from, particularly when I am eating alone, which I do too frequently. Eating is too often for me just a way of fueling up, and not a sacrament.

I appreciate that Judaism prescribes blessings as a way to ritualize the eating process and remind me of the miracle of food. When I remember to offer a blessing, for a split second, I am able to tune into my kinship with other creatures and the sacredness of life. I tend to make blessings more when I eat meat, because I feel particularly indebted to the animals who have given their lives so that I can better enjoy mine. Moments like these enrich my life, deepening my connection to creation and Creator.

≈≈

And to **every** beast of the earth, and to **every** flyer of the heaven, and to **every** creeper on the earth that has a living soul, **every** green grass for food." And it was so. (1.30)

*u-le-**khol**-chayat ha-aretz u-le-**khol**-of ha-shamayim*
*u-le-**khol** romais al-ha-aretz asher-bo nefesh chayah et-**kol**-yerek aisev*
le-akhlah. Va-yehi khain.

≈≈

COMPASSION FOR ANIMALS

While the seeds and the fruits are designed for people to eat, the green part of the plants, including the stems and leaves, were for the animals.[23] Unlike people, animals have the teeth and the stomach and the right kind of bacteria to digest the cellulose, the building block of plant greens. God provided for the animals the greens, which they need, just as God provided fruits and grains for people.

We tend to think that God's primary interest is in people, but as this verse indicates, God also makes a point of caring for animals. This is not the first time God expresses such caring. God dedicates one and a half days to the creation of all the animals while giving a half day to people. And just as God blesses the people, God also blesses the birds, the fish, and the land animals, promising them protection, fertility, and abundance.

The repetition of the word *khol*/every—every beast, every bird, and every creeping thing in this verse—further emphasizes God's care for the animals. It is as if God watches out for each individual creature to make sure that it gets just the right kind of food to eat in the right proportion. In catering to the needs of every single animal, God shows people the kind of special caring each creature requires.

But caring for others has never been easy for humanity. The very first people, Adam and Eve, and their progeny were preoccupied with their own immediate gratification and cared for little outside themselves. They would destroy themselves and their world before looking out for others.

It has been suggested that the first person to demonstrate real caring was Noah. According to Aviva Zornberg, Noah's experience in the ark with all the animals was like a "kindness" intensive. With nothing elase to distract him, Noah could grapple with his own self-centeredness and learn to cultivate the generous behaviors necessary to insure the future of life on earth. "For twelve months in the ark," the rabbis wrote, "he had not a wink of sleep, neither by day nor by night, for he was occupied in feeding the creatures who were with him."[24] He painstakingly chose the food that each species liked and he fed each one at the time at which it was accustomed.[25]

Noah's story has important ramifications for us today. As Noah committed himself to the animals and engaged in their lives, they become an integral part of his; he would never again see them as a burden outside of himself. He learned to intuit their needs, and derived pleasure and meaning in responding to them. Caring for other creatures became a privilege and an opportunity rather than a burden.[26]

The environmental crisis is founded in apathy. We have lost the ability to care for anything outside of ourselves. The psalmist cries out, "Teach us to number our days." Teach us to live each day fully, knowing that our time on earth is measured. Teach us to open our hearts to other people and creatures, to deepen our humanity and our sense of community. The more we care, the more meaningful our lives become.

And God saw everything that God had made and look! it was **very good.** And there was evening and there was morning, the sixth day. (1.31)

*Va-yar Elohim et-kol-asher asah ve-hinaih-**tov meod.***
Va-yehi-erev va-yihi-voker yom hashishi.

GOODNESS, INTERDEPENDENCE, WHOLENESS

The familiar refrain is repeated for the last time, only here, God sees the creation as "very good." On the sixth day, God designs the land creatures, creates the first human couple, and completes the entire creation. In and of itself, an individual creation may be good, but when it can contribute to a larger interdependent ecosystem, it is very good. The whole is greater than the sum of the parts.

The goodness of this day is further emphasized through the language used to describe it. While all the other days are referred to as "a" day, the sixth day is referred to as "the" day. This day is distinguished among all the rest: it is whole. Wholeness rests in the complete web of life.

Both from an ecological perspective and from Genesis' point of view, goodness resides in the community, the web of life, in the relations of the whole biosphere. All organisms interact constantly with their surroundings, in an endless cycle of giving and receiving. No creature, human or otherwise, can live in isolation. "No matter how sophisticated and complex and powerful our institutions," said Wendell Berry, "we are still exactly as dependent on the earth as the earth worms." Ultimately our individual happiness rests on the health and well-being of the larger earth ecosystem and the common good.

Goodness does not just necessarily mean "beneficial" to humanity or to an individual species or community. Water can come as torrential rains that destroy crops or as life-giving rains that insure food for the multitudes; wind can bring plagues and pestilence as well as fresh air; fire can burn down a forest and can reinvigorate a forest; earth can be rugged and intractable or fertile and nourishing. Water, air, fire, earth, plants, and animals—in their various moods and conditions—are all "good," all beloved creations of the Creator.

The "bad" in something appears when we misuse or abuse it. For example, if we remove a creation from its web, and introduce it to a new environment—take purple loosestrife for example—it can multiply out of hand and become a pest, overtaking habitats and crowding out all the native plants.

If we believe that we stand at the center of life and that the world revolves around us, then we can perceive things as "bad." If things don't go the way we want, we say that they're "bad." But there is no such thing as "bad" from God's perspective; it is all one;

all good. Ultimately our well-being and our sense of "goodness" involves learning about God's creation and adapting to it, rather than assuming it should adjust to us.

Nature is not benevolent; nature speaks truth and is just. Nature doesn't make exceptions, doesn't play favorites, "never tempers her decrees with mercy. And in the end is this not best?" wrote naturalist John Burroughs. "Could the universe be run as a charity or as a benevolent institution or as a poorhouse . . . ?"[27] It is a hard truth, but rocks are hard and they form the foundation of the world and provide stone for shelter.

THE SABBATH

THE SEVENTH DAY

And the heaven and the earth
were finished, and all their hosts.

By the seventh day, God finished the work
which God had been doing,
and on the seventh day God ceased
from all the work which God had done.

And God blessed the seventh day
and made it holy,
because on it God ceased from all work,
that God created to make.

❧

The heavens and the earth were finished, and all of their **hosts** (2.1)

*Va-yekhulu ha-shamayim ve ha-aretz ve khol-**tzevaam**.*

❧

CREATION AND THE SYNAGOGUE/CHURCH: EARTHLY HOSTS?

Maimonides says that the *tzevaam*, which is often translated as "array," or multitude refers to all the beasts, creepers, fish, growing things, and people. The word *tzeva* literally means host or army, an organized and disciplined body dedicated to carrying out its leader's will. While the luminaries and the angels are the hosts of the heavens, the creatures are hosts of the earth. Adam and Eve and all the creatures are earthly hosts performing God's work on the ground.

When I think of the various meanings of the word *tzevaam*, I imagine an army of earth citizens coming together on behalf of the diverse multitudes of creation. The obvious place to look for such an army is the organized religious community, but we would have to search hard to find something resembling a body of earth citizens here. Churches and synagogues traditionally have kept their distance from environmental affairs and the care of creation.

The schism between religious institutions and nature has deep historical roots. Christianity and Judaism evolved within and adapted to human-made cities, not in the open air of the countryside in the presence of God's awesome creation. Religious institutions struggled to distinguish themselves from the nature religions of the peasants and dedicated themselves to human nature and the human's place in society (not in nature).

This combination of a fear of nature and nature-based religions and a primary interest in human concerns and social issues undoubtedly did much to turn the religious establishment away from nature. In exiling nature from our houses of worship, we have also exiled God, and we have done a profound disservice to the earth. But it need not be this way.

Alan Watts captured the incongruency of this situation in the early 1950s:

> It has been my impression that there is a deep and quite extraordinary incompatibility between the atmosphere of Christianity and the atmosphere of the natural world. . . . I have been puzzled by the fact that I can feel like a Christian only when I am indoors. As soon as I get into the open air, I feel entirely out of relation with everything that goes on in a church including both the worship and the theology. . . . If God made this world how is it possible to feel so powerful a difference of style between the God of church and altar, for all his splendor, and the world of the open sky?[1]

While religious institutions have distanced themselves from creation in the past, there is no reason for this attitude to continue. So many elements of the religious life beckon us to connect to creation as a way to experience the Divine. Our liturgies reflect the attitudes of the psalmist, who was undeniably intoxicated with nature and saw it as a manifestation of God's work. The Bible, a story of a people in relationship with their land, provides opportunities for us to explore our connections and responsibility to nature through the weekly readings. The agricultural dimension of the holy days offer the unique flavors of each season.

It's not just the texts and rituals that ask us to honor creation, the very fabric of Jewish life brings us face to face with creation on a regular basis. Judaism's restriction on driving on Shabbat encourages people to live close enough to synagogue that they can walk there. A walking life offers opportunities to appreciate creation on a daily basis. For me as a child, the best part of the synagogue experience was walking there. Today, walking still characterizes my Shabbat experience: walking to *shul* (synagogue) in the morning, walking to lunch afterwards, and a long lingering walk in the woods to round out the perfect day.

With a little effort, we can begin to integrate ecological sensibilities into religious life and turn our churches and synagogues into gathering places for *tzevaam*. Some synagogues and churches have taken on various environmental behaviors by purchasing environmentally sound products and alternative energy and supporting various environmental causes. What is more difficult is overcoming the fears, prejudices, and petrified ideas that have created the rift between religion and nature in the first place and cultivating an abiding love for nature.

It is time for religious institutions to do the inner work that must be done to rise to the challenge of this environmental age. It is time to honor the Creator by honoring the creation.

➥

By the seventh day, God **finished** the work which God
had been doing,
and on the seventh day God **ceased** from all the work which God
had done. (2.2)

*Va-**yekhal** Elohim ba-yom ha-shevi'i melakhto asher asah
va-**yishbot** ba-yom ha-shevi'i mi-kol melakhto asher asah.*

➥

THE BALANCE OF WORK AND REST

The number seven appears more than five hundred times in the Bible. In addition to the weekly cycle, Shavuot fall seven weeks after Passover, the sabbatical year comes around every seventh year, and the Jubilee comes every forty-ninth year (seven sevens). Seven also expresses the idea of perfection and the conclusion of a cycle.

The seventh day, like the first and fourth, is concerned with time. God created day, on the first day, calendrical time on the fourth day, and rest, the release from ordinary time, on the seventh day. The seventh day also marks the creation of the first week. Many theologians claim that the week is the only unit of time that has no special relation to the natural world. They argue that while "day" is determined by the earth's rotation, "month" by the moon's cycle around the sun, and "year" by the earth's cycle around the sun, the "week" finds its origin in the biblical creation story. This position seems to overlook the fact that the week marks one quarter of the moon's monthly cycle. The week is a fundamental expression of nature's cycles and the Sabbath honors this elemental connection.

With the seventh day, the heavens and earth and the whole earthly array of creatures were complete. On each day, God designed a new piece of the creation. On the seventh day, there was nothing more to do. Anything else would be excessive and would detract from the masterpiece that God had already made. Having created "enough," God stopped.

On the seventh day, God finished working/*yekhal*, and rested/*yishbot*. It's impossible to rest and work at the same time. Work and rest are opposites; they demand different states of mind and heart. By setting a boundary on the work of the physical creation, God opened the way for rest.

Yishbot, "(God) ceased," is related to the word, Sabbath, Shabbat, the day of rest, and to the words seven, *sheva*, and sit, *yoshev*. Each of these words point to the meaning of the seventh day. On the seventh day, God ceased work, sat down, contemplated, and received. On the seventh day, God stepped off the Director's throne and fell in love with the world. On the seventh day God dwelled in the creation, engaged with all the creatures, and found pleasure and contentment in everything.

Like the other creations, rest requires its own day. Rest is not a negative concept; it is not the absence of work; it is inherently positive. While God's work yielded tangible gifts on the first six days—earth, water, planets, fish—God's rest brought intangible gifts on the seventh—time, rest, soul, serenity, peace, relationships.

The pattern of six days of work and one day of rest established a rhythm with its own integrity, providing an infrastructure for a rich and meaningful life. Work and rest are complementary parts of the cycle. Six days work, one day rest; six days using time, one day letting time be; six days mastery, one day surrender.

We are charged by the Bible to live according to creation's cycle by observing the Sabbath; "Six days you shall work, but the seventh is a Sabbath to the Lord: you shall do no work—neither you nor your children, nor your slaves, nor your animals."[2]

During the work-week, the world exists for us to use. Work can be wonderful and fulfilling, particularly if our labor reflects who we are. For many of us, our occupations give our lives meaning and provide a sense of self-worth.

On the other hand, it is possible to become slaves to our industry. Even those of us who love our work can have a hard time resting. When work becomes a means to an end, when we "use" time to create money, we too are used. Many of us hurry through our lives, dividing time into ever smaller increments and stuffing more activities into our days, expecting more from ourselves, from each other, and from nature. We can become so habituated to this situation that we do not recognize that through our work we dominate nature and grow separated from it. We are starved for rest and so is nature.

The Sabbath can be the antidote to the lifestyle of escalating demands. "The Sabbath dissolves the artificial urgency of our days," writes author Wayne Muller.[3]

To actually receive the Sabbath, we must create space for it in our lives; we must build what Jewish philosopher A. J. Heschel called a "palace in time."

> Six days a week we live under the tyranny of things of space; on the Sabbath we try to become attuned to holiness in time. It is a day on which we are called upon to share in what is eternal in time, to turn from the results of creation to the mystery of creation, from the world of creation to the creation of the world.[4]

Just because there's one day for rest and six for work doesn't mean that the day of rest is less important than the others. The re-

ceptive quality of Sabbath rest balances the controlling tempera-
ment of the six working days. The rabbis said that all the days existed for the sake of the Sabbath. Conversely, when we infuse the
week with the Sabbath vision, we can lift up the other days to
a holy purpose. Work becomes more meaningful in the context
of rest.

From God's point of view, the Sabbath is so important that it
occupies a hallowed place in our moral system as one of the Ten
Commandments. Keeping the Sabbath is a requirement for an ethi-
cal life—just as important as not killing, stealing, or committing
adultery. Keeping the Sabbath, making time for ourselves, for love,
relationship, community, and the creation, is necessary for a good
and just society. Violating the Sabbath, like breaking any of the
Commandments, leads to the unraveling of the fabric of our culture. It's just that the effects of the violation of the Sabbath are
more insidious. They include societal ills and stress-related diseases
that develop so slowly that we don't associate them with our disre-
gard for rest.

The Sabbath commandment is the only one of the ten that bids
us to "remember," as if God knows we will forget. Remember to
take the time to honor all the gifts of creation that the Sabbath com-
memorates; remember to delight in life and all of its fruits; remember to rest and replenish and nourish yourself.

We are also told to "observe" the Sabbath. Observe, as if we're
seeing for the first time. Witness the day. Watch all the creatures;
become intimate with your surroundings; take walks in the woods;
care for it. Observe the Sabbath; keep it holy: do not interfere with
its integrity.

The rabbis elaborated on the meaning of Shabbat-keeping
and rest by examining the idea of work. Many of us think of work
as what we do to make a living; the exertion of mental or physical
effort. Physical labor such as carpentry is clearly work. But work,
according to the rabbis, also includes other more subtle forms of
effort like boiling water, writing, or weeding a garden. The rabbis
described thirty-nine categories of work.

The main categories of labor are forty less one:

sowing, plowing, reaping, binding sheaves, threshing, winnowing, sorting, grinding, sifting, kneading, baking;

shearing wool, washing it, beating it, dyeing it, spinning, weaving, making two loops, weaving two threads, separating two threads, tying, untying, sewing two stitches, tearing;

trapping a deer, slaughtering it, skinning it, salting it, curing its hide, scraping it, cutting it up, writing two letters, erasing in order to write two letters;

building, tearing down, putting out a fire, kindling a fire, striking with a hammer, taking anything from one domain to another.[5]

While these categories are traditionally understood as activities associated with building the tabernacle in the desert, scholar Dr. Robert Goldenberg teaches that you can divide these thirty-nine categories of work into four broad groups: preparing food (the first eleven) making clothing (the next thirteen), producing parchment out of leather for writing (the next nine), and constructing shelter (the last six). Work, then, is defined broadly as anything that derives from these four fundamental dimensions of daily life—namely: cooking, sewing, writing, and building.

If you examine the rabbis' list closely, work literally refers to any activity that uses nature. For example, on the Sabbath, we're asked to refrain from any activities that use fire, either directly or indirectly. This means no cooking, no driving (burns gasoline), no electricity (burns fuels at source); no human generated fire, period. When we use fire we are using nature. Any human use of fire, no matter how indirect, violates nature and the spirit of the Sabbath.

We're not supposed to build on the Sabbath; that includes no repairs. Nor are we supposed to carry. Carrying anything, even if it's an umbrella or some wood, can intervene with our direct experience of nature or can lead to our use of nature. The same is true of writing and sewing.

We're asked to refrain from exchanging money on the Sabbath. Using money to buy things assumes that nature is a commodity that can be divided up and purchased. No money exchange means no counting; no breaking things apart.

In our work-day lives, we use nature as a matter of course. As we use nature, we behave as if nature revolves around us and that nature is ours to master and control. Carrying wood implies ownership of wood. Kindling fire implies ownership of fuel and all of the energy it provides. "The function of the Sabbath," wrote Mordechai Kaplan "is to prohibit humans from engaging in work which in any way alters the environment so that we should not delude ourselves into the belief that we are complete masters of our destiny."[6]

Shabbat consciousness discourages us from seeing nature's produce in terms of ourselves and therefore helps us overcome our sense of power over it and separation from it. When we give up a sense of ownership of nature, we can enter into a more conscious and intimate relationship with nature and with God. This is what is being asked of us on the Sabbath: to carry nothing, to burn nothing, to do nothing, only to "be" with God and God's creation.

The Sabbath teaches us to care for something we can never possess. It bids us to reinhabit the world, to play in creation. It encourages us to delight in all of life's visible and invisible treasures. On the Sabbath, we are a part of, not apart from creation. On the Sabbath nature is whole, indivisible, one.

The Sabbath demonstrates the power of limits inherent in the creation's design. Through its inviolability, Shabbat becomes the centerpiece of an ecologically sound life, a weekly reminder of how to live in a way that honors the creation and our selves.

People unfamiliar with the Sabbath often interpret its boundaries —no fire, no electricity, no commerce—as negative restrictions; but for anyone who observes the Shabbat, these guidelines offer freedom. The day is so rich and full that there is nowhere to drive, nothing to buy, nothing to do. Using the products of nature would only interfere with our total enjoyment of it; the day is whole and perfect as it is. The Sabbath resanctifies the creation, protecting it from human use and abuse for twenty-five hours.

It has always interested me that many environmentalists advocate abstaining from "using" nature one day a week in order to heighten our appreciation of it. They say: "Turn off the phone; put away your electrical gadgets; don't drive; don't interfere with life's natural processes; keep one day as an island in time." They believe that a ritual practice can help teach people how to live lives that honor nature. They say that without a practice that teaches us to stop, we will inevitably succumb to the societal pressures that promote faster, consumer-driven lives that exploit nature. It seems to me that these environmentalists are reinventing the Sabbath.

A midrash says that keeping the Sabbath is more important than all the other mitzvot. It says that if all of Israel would keep just one Sabbath, the messiah would come and peace would reign throughout the land. If we take the Sabbath seriously by meditating on creation, refraining from the use of nature, nurturing ourselves and our communities, loving our friends and family, we would build a sustainable world, one that could herald the messianic age.

Environmentalists have made a slogan of Aldo Leopold's words, "In wilderness is the preservation of the world." Wilderness preservation requires an army of earth citizens to do the real work of caring and preserving. What rings truer to me is a complementary slogan: In the Sabbath is the preservation of the world.

❧

And God **blessed** the seventh day and made it **holy**,
because on it God ceased from all the work,
that **God created to make.** (2.3)

*Va-**yevarekh** Elohim et-yom ha-shevi'i va-yi**kadaish** oto
ki vo shavat mi-kol-melakhto
asher-**bara Elohim la'asot.***

❧

GIVING AND RECEIVING

While on all the other days God creates, on the seventh day, God blesses. A blessing is the sweetest gift that can God give. Just as the moving creatures and the human creatures are blessed with fertility and bounty, so the hours of the seventh day are blessed with abundance. The Hebrew word *yevarekh*, bless, is related to the Hebrew word *brekha*, pool (b and v are interchangeable). The seventh day, Shabbat, is a wellspring, a fountain of blessing, infusing the world with holiness.

Through God's blessing, the seventh day becomes "holy." It took six days for God to create the world, but without the blessing of the seventh day the world would be a shell with no soul. In Exodus, it is written, "And on the seventh day God rested, *yinafash*."[7] *Nafash* means both soul and rest. On the seventh day God rested, sanctified the day, and gave the world a soul.

It's not just the world that is blessed on the seventh day; we are all blessed: on Shabbat, we are each given an additional soul, a *neshamah yetaerah*.[8] We can't receive the gift of the Shabbat soul unless we open to it. If I am too preoccupied with myself, too full of myself, then there's no space for the Shabbat soul to inhabit me.

Maimonides says that the word *shavat*, which means to cease, also means to cease talking. On the seventh day, after six days of pronouncements and spoken blessings, God stops talking and offers a silent blessing that makes the world holy. There is an inherent connection between silence, holiness, and Shabbat.

We need to nurture a kind of quietude, a kind of vacuum inside so that we can attract the *neshama yetaerah*, the holy Shabbat soul, to come and live inside us. Silence is an inner condition, not just an outer one. Just as we need to be silent in order to hear another's voice, so we need to silence the voices in our head if we want to attune ourselves to the subtle nuances of nature and the soul. Even when we are not talking out loud, we are often talking to ourselves—doubting, judging, jumping to conclusions. In such a mind, there is no room for surprises, no room for mystery, no room for holiness.

Silence invites us to watch without critiquing and comparing. If we can silence the ego, then we can learn to just be, at peace with ourselves exactly as we are and content with creation as it is.

Just as we cultivate the soil with air to give the roots of a plant space to grow, so we can cultivate the mind with silence to give the mind space to expand. A silent mind leads to a wide-open mind, a playing field where anything is possible, where wisdom and acceptance can grow.

Whereas I used to go to the woods to find silence, lately I've been finding silence where I least expected to—in *shul*/synagogue. For most of my life I was not a *shul*-goer. Even when I began to keep Shabbat in my idiosyncratic way, the religious service felt foreign to me—too many heavy, uncomfortable words, too many references to an ancient world that I did not relate to, and too much sitting. Like Alan Watts I couldn't find the Creator indoors. Now I have a different experience of *shul*. I like to find a sunny spot in the sanctuary and just sit there, letting the words wash over me. The prayers function like a kind of sacred architecture: hallowing space and inducing a meditative state.

Now I experience *shul* as the place to practice being, not doing. This is still not altogether easy for me because I'm often so uncomfortable doing nothing that *shul* seems boring. My mind is jumpy unless it's being entertained. But this pure being, this rest; this is the holiness that my soul longs for.

While we need a wide-open mind to receive the blessings of an additional soul, of love and abundance that come with holy rest, my friend Gershon says we also need a "spout" to give them away. He tells me that, according to the kabbalists, the original world shattered in order to open it up to the flow of giving and receiving. Gifts are meant to be constantly in flow—constantly "consumed" (not hoarded) and given away. If I am not in the habit of generosity, then the holiness or the Shabbat soul won't enter me because there is nowhere for it to move. The blessing, the holiness, the flow, seeks an open channel.

Problems arise when the flow gets stopped up, when giving and receiving get out of whack. It's easy to hold back from giving and withdraw into ourselves, when we don't experience the generosity flowing towards us. Many of us, afraid that there will not be enough and that we have nothing to give, live lives based in scarcity, on taking and hoarding, fortifying ourselves outwardly instead of nourishing ourselves inwardly. The environmental crisis is founded on too much taking, and not enough giving and receiving.

I now see the *shul* experience as a way to enter into the flow of giving and receiving. What Native Americans do by sprinkling tobacco on the earth in return for taking something from it, we do on Shabbat through our prayers and through our delight and through everything we do in the name of rest.

From a practical perspective, a Shabbat service only works through generosity. A Shabbat service requires participation from the community—reading from the Torah, offering a few words of wisdom, leading prayers, making lunch. There is no mercenary motive—we just rest together in the presence of each other and God. Practiced in community, the service bonds us to each other, to God, and to creation, completing the cycle of giving and receiving.

The creation story closes with an odd phrase: "God ceased from all the work that *God created to make*." In other words, God created the world so that it would keep on giving. The creation is at its core generative. Fertility, abundance, and generosity are the signature of our world.

God put all of the systems in place, insuring that the masterpiece of creation could sustain itself, and then stepped out of the way. Nature knows everything it needs to continue in perpetuity.

We need to learn from nature and respect its ability to take care of itself and provide for us, without our constant interference. We need to trust the essential rhythm of life: working and resting, doing and being, giving and receiving. We can emulate creation's ethic when we invite Shabbat into our lives. It is a powerful way to participate in creation's organic flow and to help insure the promise of God's perfect design.

✦

One glorious chain of love, of giving and receiving,
unites all things.
All things exist in continuous reciprocal activity—
one for All, All for one.
None has power, or means for itself;
Each receives only in order to give, and gives in order
    to receive,
And finds therein the fulfillment of the purpose of
    existence—HaShem.
"Love," say the Sages,
  Love that supports and is supported in return—
  that is the character of the universe.[9]

—Rabbi Samson Raphael Hirsch

✦

ENDNOTES

INTRODUCTION

1. Bahya Ibn Pakuda, *Duties of the Heart*, trans. Moses Hyamson (New York: Feldheim, 1970), 137.

CHAPTER 1

1. Some sages suggest that "earth" here refers to the universe; others say that this "earth" means planet earth, while others imagine that "earth" here refers to the element earth. Rabbi Meir Zlotowitz, transl., ed., *Bereishis* (Brooklyn: Mesorah Publications, 1986), 34.

2. Nachmanides, *Commentary on the Torah*, transl. Rabbi Dr. Charles Chavel (New York: Shilo Publishing House, 1971), Genesis I:2.

3. Gerald Shroeder, *Genesis and the Big Bang* (New York: Bantam Books, 1991), 94.

4. S. R. Hirsch, *Hirsch Humash: The Penateuch* (London: Isaac Levy Publisher, 1963), Genesis I:3.

5. Louis Ginzberg, *Legends of the Bible* (Philadelphia: Jewish Publication Society, 1992), 29.

6. Freema Gottlieb, *The Lamp of God* (Northvale, N.J.: Jason Aronson, 1989), 169.

7. Midrash Tanhuma Parshat Pekudei 3.

8. Lawrence Kushner, *River of Light* (New York: Harper and Row, 1981), 279.

9. Annie Dillard, *Pilgrim at Tinker Creek* (New York: Bantam Books, 1974), 16–17.

10. John Moyne and Coleman Barks, transl., *Open Secret: Versions of Rumi* (Putney, Vt: Threshold Books, 1984), 6, #82.

11. Hirsch, *Hirsch Humash*, Genesis I:4.

12. Robert Johnson, *Owning Your Own Shadow* (San Francisco: HarperSanFrancisco, 1991), 19.

CHAPTER 2

1. Whether or not the planet earth has been created yet is ambiguous. The word earth has been used several times and the meanings are various. For the purpose of this reading, we will assume that by second day, the planet earth has formed. The earth referred to on the third day is dry land. When the sun and moon and planets are created on the fourth day, it appears that planet earth had already been established.

The water described on the second day is likely in a more primeval state, given that the oceans as we know them were not created until the third day.

2. Ezekiel 1:22–26.

3. Ibn Ezra commentary quoted in Zlotowitz, *Bereishis*, I:6.

4. Lyall Watson, *Heaven's Breath* (Great Britain: Hodder and Stroughton, 1984), 20.

5. Ibid.

6. Ibid., 318.

7. Edward Wilson, *The Diversity of Life* (Cambridge, Mass.: Harvard University Press, 1992).

8. David Abram, *The Spell of the Sensuous* (New York: Pantheon, 1996), 236.

9. Various schools of kabbalists talk about either four or five levels of the soul; the system is basically the same in either case; one school just has an extra (higher) soul level.

CHAPTER 3

1. Ecclesiastes 1:7.

2. Thomas Schwenk, *Sensitive Chaos* (New York, Schocken Books, 1976), 14.

3. Water maintains a measured pace: when it moves at excessive speed it vaporizes; when it slows to motionless, it crystallizes.

4. Terry Tempest Williams, *An Unspoken Hunger* (New York: Vintage, 1994), 57.

5. Hirsch, *Hirsch Humash*, Genesis I:9.

6. Nachmanides, *Commentary on the Torah*, Genesis I:10.

7. Exodus 3:5.

8. Jeremiah 4:28, Leviticus 18:25, Joel 2:21, Isaiah 35:1.

9. The Egyptian land from which the Israelites fled was possessed, manipulated, and exploited.

10. Leviticus 25:23.

11. James Lovelock, *The Ages of Gaia* (New York: Bantam, 1988), 5.

12. William Bryant Logan, *Dirt* (New York: Riverhead Books, 1995), 96.

13. Rachel Carson, *Silent Spring* (New York: Houghton Mifflin, 1962), 42.

14. Nachmanides, *Commentary on the Torah*, Genesis I:11.

15. Hirsch, *Hirsch Humash*, Genesis I:11. (Plants without stamens and pistils do not bear seeds and are the most primitive of the plants). Were we to understand the earth to mean the entire surface of the planet including the seas, then blue green algae, the first organisms that covered the ancient sea, fit nicely into the *deshe* category as well.

Dr. Norbert Samuelson suggests that "earth" in this verse refers to the entire surface of the earth including the seas. Norbert Samuelson, *The First Seven Days* (Atlanta, Georgia: Scholars Press, 1992).

16. Biologist Lynn Margulis fondly describes bacteria as "metabolically gifted"; they can trap light, photosynthesize, swim, bring about decay, produce alcohol, provoke fermentation and fix nitrogen. Lynn Margulis and Dorion Sagan, *What is Life?* (New York: Simon and Schuster, 1995), 69, 72.

17. Umberto Cassuto, *A Commentary on the Book of Genesis*, trans. Israel Abrahams (Jerusalem: Magnes Press, 1961), Genesis I:10–12.

18. While the grasses grew in the valleys and on the plains, the fruit trees occupied the hills. Fruit trees provided oil, energy, utensils, furniture, building materials, wine, and fruits for eating.

19. Orchid and grass seeds are light as dust and are easily blown about, while the "wings" of maple seeds and the "parachutes" of milkweed keep them aloft. Still others, like coconuts, are specially adapted to life on the seas—they are designed with air spaces to keep them afloat.

20. A plant, struggling to survive, channels its energy into its seeds and its future.

21. Nachmanides, *Commentary on the Torah*, Genesis I:11.

22. "Just as God needs the blade of grass and the cedar tree . . . in His household of the world and gives each its law—in the faithful fulfillment of which each joyfully lives its appointed life so that it can happily and faithfully make its contribution to the whole without worrying about why it is a blade of grass and not a cedar tree, why corn and not vine, leaving the plan of the world to God—in the same way God has given to each individual person his special calling and the law. The continued existence of the species is essentially dependent on maintaining its integrity and every non-observance of God's law digs a grave for the species." Hirsch, *Hirsch Humash*, Genesis I:13.

23. Judith Soule and Jon Piper, *Farming in Nature's Image* (Washington, D.C.: Island Press, 1992), 11.

24. Rifkin, Jeremy, *The Biotech Century* (New York: Tarcher Books (Penguin/Putnam), 1998).

25. Robert Rhoades, "The World's Food Supply at Risk," *National Geographic* (April 1991), 74–101.

26. Donella Meadows, "Poor Monsanto," *Whole Earth* (Summer 1999), 104.

27. Rifkin, *The Biotech Century*, 110.

28. Louis Ginzberg, *Legends of the Jews* (Philadelphia: Jewish Publication Society, 1992), 9.

29. Ibid., 10.

30. Evan Eisenberg, *The Ecology of Eden* (New York: Knopf, 1997), 99.

31. Ezekial 47:7–12.

32. Quoted by Terry Tempest Williams in *An Unspoken Hunger* (New York: Vintage, 1994), 74.

33. Thomas Hylton, *Save Our Lands, Save Our Towns* (Harrisburg, Pa.: RB Books, 1995), 17.

34. Philo, commentary on Genesis quoted in Zlotowitz, *Bereishis*, Genesis I.13.

35. Quoted by Scott Russel Saunders in *Staying Put* (Boston, Beacon Press, 1993), 120.

36. Sara Stein, *Noah's Garden* (Boston: Houghton Mifflin, 1993), 17.

CHAPTER 4

1. Other creation stories follow the same sequence as the biblical one. Noted here is the "Metamorphoses of Ovid":

> Whichever god it was, he thus divided
> that formless heap, distributing its members,

first modeling the mighty ball of earth . . .
then ordering seas to spread and swell with rushing
winds and encompass shores around the earth . . .
He bids the plains expand, the valleys sink,
forests grow leaves, and rocky mountains rise. . . .
Scarcely had he thus given all things limits,
when constellations, long oppressed by darkness,
suddenly effervesced throughout the sky.
Lest any region be deprived of life,
stars and divine forms occupied the heavens,
waters became the shiny fishes' homes,
earth received beasts and fluttering air the birds.

"The Metamorphoses of Ovid," trans. Robert M. Torrence, in *Encompassing Nature* (Washington, D.C.: Counterpoint, 1998), 473.

2. Hirsch, *Hirsch Humash*, Genesis I:14. Although the idea of time is introduced on day one with the creation of light and the concept of "day," time is not set in motion until the fourth day when the light-bearers, the sun and the moon and the planets, are created.

3. Mark Twain, "Was the World Made for Man," in *Collected Tales, Sketches, Speeches & Essays*, ed. Louis J. Budd (New York: Library of America, 1992).

4. Daniel Bremen and John O'Conner, *Who Owns the Sun* (White River Junction, Vt.: Chelsea Green Publishing, 1996), 66.

5. Linnaeus Flower Clock, Martin & Anna's website, www.users .globalnet.co.uk/~sykesm/aboutFlowerClock.html.

6. The Lakota encourage the women to follow the "Grandmother moon": to be outwardly active and creative when she is at her brightest and most open. When the Grandmother begins to cover her face, the Lakota say its time for the women to withdraw into a quieter, less social place. In the dark of the moon, when bleeding, the veil between women and the Great Mystery is nearly transparent. This is the time to be receptive to visions and intuition, so it is best to separate oneself and rest in a Moon Lodge. When the moon returns, it is time for the woman to come out of the dark with a cleansed body and a new vision.

7. The standard translation of the verb *natan* in this context is put or placed; I have translated literally.

8. Mishnah Berakhot 9:2.

9. Rab Judah said in the name of Samuel: To enjoy anything of this world without offering a blessing is like making personal use of things consecrated to heaven, since it says, "The earth is the Lord's and the fullness thereof" (Psa. 24:1), Babylonian Talmud Berakhot 35a–35b.

10. In the year 540 the monk Benedict wrote a guide to proper worship known as the Benedictine rule.

11. This prayer is recited in the morning; a slightly different version is recited in the evening.

CHAPTER 5

1. The standard translation for *nefesh* here is creatures; I have translated literally, using the word "soul."

2. Babylonian Talmud Hullin 127a; Midrash Yalkhut Shimoni, 862.

3. The best swimmers are spindle-shaped, round in the middle and tapered at either end. Tuna, swordfish and dolphin have the ideal body type for moving through water with the least effort. Projections along the body create additional drag so expert swimmers reduce or eliminate any appendages they don't need for swimming and steering. They have no external ears, no nipples, no neck. Their fins are also spindle shaped rather than being long and lanky like our arms and legs. They are symmetrical and streamlined to cut through the water with ease.

4. Bereishit Rabbah, I:20.

5. While *yivra/bara* refers to the creation of something fundamentally new, and may be alluding to the *tanninim*, it may also be referring to animals or to independent movement itself.

6. Rashi, Nachmanides, *Commentary on the Torah*, Genesis I:22.

7. Sforno, commentary quoted in Zlotowitz, *Bereishis*, Genesis I:22.

8. Marshall Norman, *The Life of Fishes* (New York: Universe Books, 1966).

9. Rabbi Aharon Halevi of Barcelona, Sefer HaHinukh, Mitzvah 294 (thirteenth century).

10. Mark McMenamin, *Scientific American*, vol. 256 (April 1987), 96.

11. David Brower, *Let the Mountains Talk; Let the Rivers Run* (San Francisco: Harper Collins, 1995), 15.

12. Ibid.

13. Bruce Chatwin, *The Songlines* (New York: Viking Penguin, 1988), 162.

14. Exodus 13:17.

15. Deuteronomy 16:16.

CHAPTER 6

1. Nachmanides, *Commentary on the Torah*, Genesis I:24.

2. Meredith Sabini, ed., *The Earth Has a Soul: The Nature Writings of C. G. Jung* (Berkeley: North Atlantic Press, 2002).

3. Bahya Ibn Pakuda, *Duties of the Heart*, trans. Moses Hyamson (New York: Feldheim, 1970), 137.

4. Norman Lamm, *Spirituality and Law in Judaism* (Philadelphia: JPS, 1998), 13–14.

5. Ibn Ezra, commentary quoted in Zlotowitz, *Bereishis*, Genesis I:26.

6. Nachmanides, *Commentary on the Torah*, Genesis I:26.

7. Vilna Gaon, commentary quoted in Zlotowitz, *Bereishis*, Genesis I:26.

8. Hirsch, *Hirsch Humash*, Genesis I:26.

9. Deuteronomy 22:6–7.

10. "You will not plow with an ox and an ass together" (Deut. 22:10).

11. Lynn White, "The Historical Roots of Our Ecological Crisis," *Science* 155, (10 March 1967).

12. Wendell Berry, environmental writer and farmer, appalled by this anti-environmental reading of Genesis, demanded, "How, for example, would one arrange to 'replenish the earth' if 'subdue' means, as alleged, 'conquer' or 'defeat' or destroy?" Berry contends: "The ecological teaching of the Bible is simply inescapable: God made the world because He wanted it made. He thinks the world is good and He loves it. It is His world; He has never relinquished title to it. . . . If God loves the world, then how might any person of faith be excused for not loving it or justified in destroying it?" Wendell Berry, *What Are People For?* (San Francisco: North Point Press, 1990), 99.

13. In all the biblical commentaries over the last two thousand years, the rabbis rarely even mentioned dominion, undoubtedly because Jews rarely owned their own land for most of history, and consequently were not in a position to dominate nature. What little the rabbis did say about dominion—most rabbinic commentary focuses on the "be fruitful" half of the verse—was framed in the context of governance of nature, never control. They compared humanity's dominion of nature on the sixth day to God's governance of the luminaries on the fourth day. Humanity's charge is to preserve the order and integrity of creation, maintaining all the diverse kinds of organisms. The prototype of dominion was Adam's stewardship of the Garden of Eden (Gen. 2:15).

14. Aviva Zornberg, *The Beginning of Desire* (Philadelphia: JPS, 1995).

15. Psalm 8:6.

16. Norbert Samuelson, *The First Seven Days* (Atlanta: Scholars Press, 1992).

17. Rashi, *Pentateuch and Rashi Commentary*, Genesis I:26.

18. Provocative verses in the Bible have generated thousands of years of rabbinic debate. But, other than the comment by Rashi, the rabbis are, by and large, silent on the question of "dominion" and "mastery of the earth." Since, throughout history, Jews were rarely allowed to own land, the rabbis undoubtedly found the idea of mastering the earth and the creatures irrelevant to their circumstances. They were more concerned that people would not be able to master their passions and their pride than that people would (improperly) master the earth and the animals. One must learn to balance oneself before taking charge of anything else.

Rather than giving humanity a mandate to control or exploit the earth, the primary object lesson of the Bible is that of humility. We need a sense of humility to balance our sense of pride. Through stories and laws, the futility of hubris is taught over and over again. The Midrash asks: "Why does God create all of the creatures before humanity? So human beings should not grow too proud. You can say to them, 'Even the gnat came before you in the Creation!'" (Tosefta Sanhedrin 8:4).

Indeed the whole book of Ecclesiastes is a commentary on the pointlessness of vanity:

> What befalls the generations of man befalls the beast . . .
> as the one dies, so the other dies.
> Yes, they all have one breath
> Man has no preeminence above the beasts
> for all is vanity
> All go to one place
> All are dust and return to dust
> Who knows the spirit of man, whether it rises up
> and the spirit of beast whether it descends below to the earth?
> (Eccl. 4:19–21)

And God's longest monologue in the entire Bible is a desperate cry of despair at the arrogance of humans:

> Can he be taken by his eyes?
> Can his nose be pierced by hooks?

Can you draw out Leviathan by a fishhook?
Can you put a ring through his nose
Or pierce his jaws with a barb?
Will he plead with you at length?
Will he speak soft words to you?
Will he make an agreement with you
To be taken as your lifelong slave?
Will you play with him like a bird and tie him down for your girls?
Shall traders traffic in him?
Will he be divvied up among merchants? (Job 40:24–30)

19. Genesis 2:15.

20. Leviticus 25:23.

21. Rav Saadia Gaon, in commentary on Genesis I:26, quoted by the Christian theologian Claus Westermann, highlights the unfolding development of a distinctively human civilization replete with technological discovery and artistic refinement. Claus Westermann, *Genesis I–II: A Commentary,* trans. John Scullion (Minneapolis: Fortress Press, 1984), 25.

22. In the beginning, the Midrash says, people and animals were vegetarians and were destined to live forever. It was only after the Flood, after people learned to care for the animals on the ark, that God gave them permission to eat meat.

23. According to Rambam, Sforno, and Targum Yonatan, this verse is a separate clause addressed to the animals. Zlotowitz, *Bereishis,* commentaries on Genesis I.30.

24. Midrash Tanhuma Parshat? 2; Zornberg, 60.

25. Bereishit Rabbah 39.

26. Similarly, many of Israel's heroes including Abel, Isaac, Moses, Jacob, and David would mature and learn the craft of leadership by caring for the animals. According to the Midrash, David, like Noah, took special pains for each sheep, directing the kids to eat the tender tops of the grass, the rams to the grass stems, and the old sheep to the roots (Midrash Shmot Rabba 2:3). In honor of his time in the fields, David composed innumerable psalms that sing praise to the life of the shepherd. Still, learning kindness has been a difficult lesson for humanity and the Bible ultimately prescribed laws to legislate kindness to animals. For example: "You will not muzzle the ox when he treads out the corn" (Deut 25:4). In other words, when your ox is working in the cornfields surrounded by the food he enjoys, you should not prevent him from eating. Similarly, "you should not

harness two species together," because the weaker animal suffers if it is obliged to keep pace with the stronger and the stronger suffers if it is restrained by the weaker (Deut 22:10). Moreover you should not even purchase a domestic animal, wild beast, or bird unless you are able to feed it properly.

27. John Burroughs, "The Gospel of Nature," in *Time and Change* (Boston: Houghton Mifflin, 1912).

CHAPTER 7

1. Alan Watts, *Nature, Man and Woman* (New York: Vintage Books, 1991), 26, 28.

2. Exodus 20:8–10.

3. Wayne Muller, *The Sabbath* (New York: Bantam Books, 1999).

4. A. J. Heschel, *The Sabbath* (New York: Farrar, Straus and Giroux, 1983), 10.

5. *Mishna* Shabbat 7:2.

6. Mordechai Kaplan, *Judaism as a Civilization* (New York: Reconstructionist Press, 1981), 443–44.

7. Exodus 31:17.

8. Zohar hadash 17b. We get an additional soul / *neshamah yetaerah* on the Shabbat. The *neshamah yetaerah* comes from the light of the first day.

9. Rabbi Samson Raphael Hirsch, Germany 1808–1888, "Third Letter," *The Nineteen Letters (1836)*, trans. Rabbi Bernard Drachman / Jacob Breuer (London: Soncino Press, 1960).